CAUGHT SHORT
By Jennifer Dodd

Disclaimer

This book is a work of non-fiction based on the life, experiences and recollections
of the author. The names of some people, places, dates, sequences or the detail of
events have been changed to protect the privacy of others.

This book is not intended as a substitute for the medical advice of physicians. The
reader should regularly consult a physician in matters relating to his/her health and
particularly with respect to any symptoms that may require diagnosis or medical
attention.

For Nan

"They may forget what you said – but they will never forget how you made them feel"
Carl W Buehner

Contents

Preface

Have you ever felt as though your entire existence revolves around the toilet? Some days I have to make this decision. Is it worth the risk, to leave the house perhaps just to get a pint of milk or walk the dog? Will I make it, or will the unthinkable happen?

The possibility that my bowels may refuse to hold on until an appropriate time is one I have to consider every single day. Sadly, this is a very real and humiliating threat for me and so many others!

I am thirty eight years old and since I was thirteen my life has been affected, to some degree by my bowels. I am just one of the growing 240,000 people diagnosed with Ulcerative Colitis (UC) or Crohn's Disease (Inflammatory Bowel Disease; [IBD]) in the UK alone. It is estimated that IBD affects about 1 person in every 250. Despite its prevalence IBD is still shrouded in shame for many sufferers, even going undiagnosed due to stigma and fear.

Although public awareness surrounding these conditions is growing there is still a huge amount of ignorance. With these aptly termed "invisible illnesses" a sufferer can look deceptively well. This coupled with a lack of understanding can lead to embarrassment and isolation. Recently there was a report of a lady with UC being refused access to a disabled toilet. The toilet attendant justified her decision by saying

"Well you don't look ill."

Living with a debilitating disease is painful so empathy and awareness are crucial!

My life with IBD has, at its best been challenging and at its worst an utter nightmare. Some of my early experiences are particularly difficult to sugar coat and were awful to walk through. As an adult my encounters in both hospital and medical environments have been easier to manage. This is partly due to the fact I have developed emotional maturity and resilience.

To give a full and honest account of my experiences both the negatives and positives need to be recognised. Some of the treatment I received following my diagnosis of UC was void of anything resembling compassion or understanding. I was expected to cope with situations and information that an adult would struggle to comprehend. There was little consideration for my immaturity and fears.

On the flip side there are numerous occasions when my care has been exemplary. The doctors and nurses who treated me with respect; gave me time to ask questions or just reassured me with a smile made a massive difference to my journey with IBD.

The National Health Service is a wonderful institution and we are so fortunate to have such wonderful health care, free at the point of contact. I am so appreciative of the medical intervention I have received throughout my life. It isn't an exaggeration to say that without it, I wouldn't have the privilege of sharing my story at all.

I have considered my motivation for writing this book quite deeply. It is very difficult to explain without sounding self-indulgent and possibly critical of those who have treated me or tried to sympathise with me. Unless you are the individual living with the pain and humiliation that is symptomatic of an IBD then it is almost impossible to comprehend.

My objective is to describe how it really feels to be a young adult growing up with an IBD; and the emotional, mental and social difficulties involved. I would like others affected by these unforgiving and humiliating diseases to perhaps feel slightly less alone.

I greatly hope to give medical professionals the perspective of a patient. To provide insight as to how it feels to be a terrified patient trapped in a clinical, unfamiliar nightmare. Without sounding arrogant or patronising; I genuinely believe that doctors and nurses are less able deliver effective care unless they possess a sincere empathy for their patients.

Finally and most importantly, I would like to give hope to those individuals who feel the torture of IBD is relentless. To offer reassurance that it is possible for things to improve. There are ways to adapt and lead a fulfilling and happy life without the shadow of these diseases defining or controlling you. However tough my life as a casualty of IBD has been, my experiences have made me the compassionate and spirited woman I am today. As clichéd as it sounds, I am exceptionally grateful for this.

So here, in all of its' painful/smelly/honest/ humorous and completely unapologetic glory is my story. If you are reading this while sitting on the loo......keep smiling xx

Prologue

I can vividly remember the first time an embarrassing "toilet situation" affected me. I was twelve years old, it was a Friday night and school were hosting the annual leavers disco.

My best friend Amy and I were having a great time, dancing and showing off. Obsessed with cheesy eighties pop we had dance routines galore and truly believed ourselves to be as hip as the professional dancers in the music videos. This slight delusion left us uninhibited and free......how well we actually performed is debatable!

There were a number of kids at the disco who didn't attend our school. It was intended as a "mixer" to integrate us in preparation for the move up to senior school. Despite this we continued to stick with our usual friend groups, eyeing up our potential new classmates from a safe distance.

I was at an age where I preferred to open my bowels in the privacy of my own home and would always try and hold on until these familiar surroundings were available. A school disco was the last place I wanted to go but my body had been subtly communicating the need for a while. As the cramps worsened it became clear that there was no other choice. Mumbling to Amy that I was going to the loo I ran to the toilets. The urgency suddenly so intense that I only just made it.

The diarrhoea that followed was a dreadful shock. I had experienced "the runs" before but this was something quite different. My insides felt as though they were in a vice and my bottom burned. The pain was so excruciating it left me nauseous. When it was over I sat still waiting for the sick feeling to ease before wiping myself clean. I jolted at the sight of blood on the toilet tissue and wondered if this was the start of my periods.

As I stood up it was obvious that the blood had come from the back not the front. The toilet was a horrible mess, diarrhoea, blood and snot like mucus filling the bowl. It was both disgusting and terrifying! With shaking hands and jelly legs I flushed and exited the cubicle.

My heart sank when I saw some girls in the toilets. They must have been from one of the other schools because I didn't recognise them. They were staring at me. I knew I had made a smell and my face burned with shame as I washed my hands. The dark haired girl sneered at me nastily.

'Did you crap your pants, you stink?'

The others laughed at their ringleader. I ran out of the toilets in tears, still traumatised from the painful diarrhoea, let alone the humiliation of it being noticed. The disco was over for me, I told the teacher Mrs Elson I felt poorly.

'You do look pale Jenny, let me phone your mum to come and get you,' she said.

So I left my friends dancing and was grateful when my parents arrived ten minutes later.

Mum was worried but I played down how ill I had been, pushing the horror of the bloody mess in the toilet out of my mind. Everyone has a bad tummy sometimes, right? I only prayed those girls hadn't told anyone about the awful smell I made.

It must have greatly affected me; years later and I can still picture their faces mocking me. Just kids being kids, of course, I know that now. They will never have realised the impact their taunting had on me. To them, I was just a girl who had the shits at a disco instantly forgotten as they carried on dancing and having fun.

The excitement of the summer holidays soon replaced the acute embarrassment and it was, for a while forgotten. Unfortunately and unbeknown to me this incident was the first sign of a debilitating disease which would shape my life forever.

A Little Bag of Sugar

After I received my diagnosis of Ulcerative Colitis (UC), many people asked me if it came on suddenly or if the symptoms were present during my early childhood. Were there any warning signs that the disease was lurking or any significant or traumatic events which could have led to its' development? These are questions I have pondered over many times. It is impossible to say definitively, however I believe that my disease is partly attributed to certain factors.

I was born just over two months early. A condition called Pre-Eclampsia elevated my mums' blood pressure to a dangerously high level. Feeling unwell with a blinding headache Mum had visited the doctor. It was very fortunate she did as we were both in grave danger. In the middle of explaining her symptoms Mum lost consciousness and was rushed into hospital. The only possible treatment was to deliver me, so ready or not I was to enter the world!

As a child I was fascinated by the anecdote of my dramatic birth and despite having it narrated to me numerous times was always keen to hear it again. I was delivered by Caesarean Section and weighed a tiny two pounds and eleven ounces.

There are photographs of me in the incubator resembling a helpless baby bird yet to gain its' feathers. Ugly blue veins are prominent under my translucent tissue paper skin. In the photograph Mums' hand is next to me, wanting to be close yet unable to touch me. Her index finger is only ever so slightly larger than my arm which emphasizes my tiny size. It is a powerful image.

Not expected to live I was christened very soon after birth. However, despite doctors concerns; and regardless of the fact I wasn't quite set for this world, I survived. My great grandmother affectionately titled me "her little bag of sugar" which always made me feel special.

Despite this turbulent beginning there was never any indication that my prematurity would cause me problems. Nor is there any substantial or conclusive research which correlates IBD with low birth weight babies. It certainly wasn't suggested by the doctors that my disease was in any way connected to my start in life.

My Nan believed there to be a link, adamant that a person couldn't be born so small without implications. Of course we will never know for sure; it is more of a curiosity. It is true to say, that in one way or another I have been fighting from the very moment I was born.

Compared to my younger brother Bill, a sturdy energetic lad, always a picture of health I was a sickly child. Pale and skinny, every cold, cough and bug seemed to find me. It was a running joke that I always had a tissue in my hand and a red nose.

'Here's Rudolf!' Dad would chuckle, tweaking my throbbing nose affectionately.

Regular illness meant regular absences from school. On these occasions I would stay with Nan, and although I wasn't well, I secretly loved it. The teapot and biscuit barrel were always full, the house cosy and comforting.

Nan had a unique ability which I have tried hard most of my adult life to emulate. She could put a person at ease while simultaneously making them believe they were the most important and interesting human she had ever known. She would smile warmly and say hello to everyone she passed in the street, which as a teenager I admit I found slightly embarrassing!

She said it was important to acknowledge people; that a smile or a kind word could perhaps make all the difference to someone having a bad day. It wasn't until years later when I was struggling and in pain and a stranger simply asked me if I was ok that I realised just how right she had been! (The same doesn't apply to those irritating prats who say things like "Smile, it might never happen". There is absolutely nothing in that sentence designed to make person on the receiving end feel better!)

Nan was an eccentric and although often unintentional, extremely funny. She would throw her head back and howl contagiously if something tickled her! However, if something annoyed her she was prone to explode and the dignified, kind lady would be replaced by something quite different. She even had her own unique list of expletives! I have to say my favourite was "Horses' Arse" which she once shouted very loudly in the supermarket when someone rudely bumped her trolley!

The term legend is branded about quite easily these days but there is no doubt that my Nan truly was an absolute legend! I would catch her looking at me sadly sometimes, after I was diagnosed with UC. She loathed seeing me in any pain and often said she wished it was happening to her and not me.

During my longest spell in hospital it was almost impossible to stay positive. The days were long and I was becoming increasingly frustrated and upset. Every day I would unsuccessfully try to convince the doctors that I was well enough to go home. One afternoon when the bell rang to signal the end of visiting, Nan bent down to give me a kiss and pressed something into the palm of my hand. It was a tiny ornament of a tortoise with a cheery green face.

'Slow and steady wins the race,' she whispered in my ear. Her eyes twinkled with love and understanding.

I still have the china tortoise. He has pride of place on my kitchen window; helping me through the bad days and making me smile. It has been five years since Nan passed yet she is always there, in my soul lovingly cheering me on

My two closest friends growing up were sisters called Amy and Kat. We were neighbours and met at the age of five when their pet rabbit escaped and cheekily hopped into our garden. From this moment we were inseparable and it is quite funny to think that we have a bunny rabbit to thank for over thirty years of friendship.

Opposite my house was a park, so evenings after school and summer holidays were spent playing outside on the swings or whizzing up and down on our bikes. Sometimes we would build dens in a wooded area close by and plead with our parents to let us camp out in them. Given that these flimsy hideouts usually collapsed within a couple of hours it was probably fortunate we were never given permission!

We would make up dance routines to pop songs or play with our Barbie Dolls. Amy and Kat had an extensive collection. I was secretly quite jealous but since they let me play with their dolls I got over it! One summer we had sleepovers almost every night for the entire six weeks. It didn't matter what we were doing, we always had so much fun.

It was this particular summer that their dad got a new job. He delivered sweets to all the local shops and drove a white van with "Fizz Bomb" written on the side in vivid sparkling letters. The back of this van was a child's dream! It was packed to the roof with jars and tubs of glorious sweets gleaming like vibrant jewels; instantly hypnotising us.

There was everything imaginable from creamy Murray Mints to the deliciously aromatic aniseed balls. I always went straight for the cola bottles savouring the sour then sweet bursts of flavour. It was our very own mobile Willy Wonka's Chocolate Factory! We would be watching our favourite cartoons after school listening out for the familiar chug of that van which would have us instantly salivating like Pavlov's dogs. Pushing and squealing we would race out, terrified of missing a single moment of the magical sweetie van.

'Go on then,' their dad would laugh opening the back up for us. We would gorge until we felt sick and then fill our pockets with more for later. We must have made quite a dent in his stock although no matter how many sweets we gobbled the supply seemed never ending! Believe me; no childhood is complete until you have been shut in the back of a sweet van!

As is naturally characteristic of youth, there was also the odd misadventure to contend with. I was feeble in appearance so tended to be an easy target for the bullies and bossy kids. It was always me getting a slap, sly dig or hair pulled by some cocky blighter desperate to stamp their claim as Kingpin.

One such occasion occurred when Amy and I, being fond of dogs, offered to walk an elderly neighbours' two very bouncy and extremely comical Jack Russell Terriers. Every weekend, feeling enormously grown up and important we would go and collect Candy and Lucy and take them out for a sniff and explore.

When we arrived they would be beside themselves with excitement and would show their appreciation by covering us with sloppy dog kisses. I would be sitting on the floor, laughing with delight as the two manic hounds zoomed around me. They were so fast and wired it was almost impossible to get their leads attached!

Unfortunately our dog walking fun was to be short lived. Some older girls in our neighbourhood, Carly and Michelle decided that they wanted the job instead. We stupidly chose to ignore their threats to "stop walking the dogs or else" naively hoping that they would forget about it. They finally cornered us one afternoon following school.

'Why are you still walking the dogs when we told you not to?' glowered Michelle.

There was a menacing glint in her eyes. Neither Amy nor I spoke. I realised to my frustration that I was visibly shaking. Our silence only enraged the bullies and Carly grabbed my arms and shoved me backwards into a conveniently placed blanket of brambles. Amy followed suit and landed on top of me. We were both crying in pain and humiliation as we tried to climb out; our attempts to avoid further damage from the evil brambles proving fruitless. I was pulling those damn thorns out of my body for days afterwards, each one a painful reminder that I had been unable to stand up for myself.

The older girls had stamped their authority and made it crystal clear that we were to stay away from the dogs unless we wanted to get completely battered.

'Look how white Jenny has gone, pathetic wimp,' Carly laughed, spitefully slapping my face before walking away.

The parting slap sealed the deal and it is safe to say we didn't walk the dogs again after that! We didn't tell our parents what had happened, explaining our injuries away as an accident. Eventually the experience faded into a childhood memory although for quite some time afterwards my stomach would lurch if I saw Carly and Michelle. Attempting to soothe our bruised egos, from a safe distance we were full of bravado.

'They only want to walk the dogs because they are a pair of smelly bitches!' I said boldly.

Amy laughed with me but it was a facade. We both knew that should we see our thorny enemies approaching we would run extremely fast in the opposite direction!

I was subject to this kind of youthful bullying many times as a child and young adult. This was probably because not only was I physically weak, I scared easily. At times it was impossible for me to hide my nerves and I would literally radiate fear! Of course this made me the perfect target for any insecure person needing to squash someone in order to feel better themselves.

Nan used to say I was a born worrier and it definitely showed; my nails were always bitten down to the quick and I wore a constant expression of apprehension. I would literally stress and fuss about every little thing, so it would be fair to say that interspersed in my happy and secure childhood was also a great deal of angst.

If I got told off by a teacher I would be mortified and worry for days. If I fell out with friends I would cry and not want to go to school as the situation exaggerated itself to extreme proportions of devastation inside my mind. I guess everyone just expected me to grow out of it but these behaviour traits definitely worsened during my adolescence.

I don't believe it is a coincidence that it was at this time the symptoms of UC first surfaced. Some studies suggest that there is a link between anxiety symptoms and "flare ups" of IBD, particularly UC. Others disagree suggesting the anxiety and depression are a result of the disease. I can identify with both theories; it is most certainly a double edged sword. Anxiety was a prominent feature of my life in the year leading up to my diagnosis of UC; and there have been times following diagnosis that the disease itself has caused me to become anxious and depressed.

Although I had quite a lot of absences due to illness I still enjoyed my primary school years. I always look back on those days; unoriginal as it sounds, as the best of my life. I was popular and had some great friends.

I did well in most subject areas with the exception of P.E. It is fair to say that any class which involved physical exertion was definitely not my forte! I would rather be writing an essay or solving maths problems in a cosy classroom than joining the long legged girls running muddy cross country. The idea of becoming sweaty jumping over hurdles didn't appeal in the slightest.

My least favourite day of the year was the dreaded sports day. I was never fast enough or strong enough to win anything and sadly possessed quite a defeatist attitude. I did enjoy a game of Rounders' once when I actually managed to hit the ball. Unfortunately I was so surprised to have made contact I forgot to run and was knocked out at the first post, much to the annoyance of my team! I think that was, and still is the highlight of my short lived sporting career! It simply wasn't for me.

What I really lived for was books. Nothing compares to the smell and feel of a new book. The delicious anticipation of what was waiting within those crisp white, untouched pages. I could read independently by the age of five, regularly burying myself in story books for hours on end. I would be blissfully unaware of the world around me; transported to a magical land full of adventures and fun where nothing was beyond the imagination. Pure delight!

I would read an entire book in a day if my parents didn't notice and force me out to play in the sunshine. It is no wonder I was so pale!

So aside from the odd encounter with a bully or fall out with friends these were reasonably care free and happy days. The symptoms of UC didn't begin until just after my twelfth birthday and prior to that I just remember things being good, safe somehow and for want of a better word, normal.

Teenage Dream

An early developer, I hit puberty at eleven years old. I was very self-conscious of my developing body, as all adolescents are. When my periods first began I couldn't wait to tell Amy, I felt so grown up and sophisticated. The novelty quickly wore off due to the fact my periods were always very heavy and excruciatingly painful.

Every month I would find myself doubled up in agony; a hot water bottle clutched against my tummy in a desperate attempt to ease the spiteful, cramps.

If this is what it means to be a woman you can shove it, I would think, feeling very sorry for myself.

I doubt there are many people who look back fondly at this time of change. Puberty is a confusing experience. Unfortunately soaring alongside my hormone levels were increasing issues with anxiety. I began suffering with severe panic attacks although had no idea that what I was experiencing had a name or cause.

One Saturday evening I was at home with my family; we were watching a hospital drama. A character of a young girl unluckily met her grizzly demise in a car crash. In a later scene, a doctor was breaking the news that she had died to her parents. The girl's mother began screaming and shouting that it couldn't be true, that it was impossible as she had only seen her daughter a few hours ago. It was extremely sad and dramatic.

All of a sudden I felt this sense of unease creep over me and a terrifying thought popped into my mind......*you are going to die tomorrow.*

In that moment, it seemed I had become painfully aware of my own mortality. Not only that, it felt like an imminent threat! The programme finished and the credits rolled, appearing blurred as terror filled me. I wanted to cry, I felt so fearful. Even now if I hear the title music associated with that particular programme, all of those emotions come flooding back.

The realisation that I could suddenly die seemed to stick within my mind. It developed further when I began to worry that someone I loved would suddenly be killed in an accident. It would play out like a graphic movie scene in my head. These terrifying thoughts would appear with no warning. Instantly I would feel like I couldn't breathe, my hands would tingle and my palms would sweat. Everything around me seemed to be moving in slow motion, surreal somehow.

It all felt so silly and embarrassing. Mum and Dad were aware that I had worries but I managed to keep the extent of them hidden too ashamed to disclose what was going on. What would they think of me if they knew the awful things I was thinking?

Then a new fear began to grow; this one involved a house fire breaking out during the night. In which my family and I would be trapped and burnt alive. The images in my mind were so vivid and explicit it almost felt as though it was actually happening. The terror induced by these thoughts would paralyze me until eventually; it began forcing me into rituals of obsessive checking. I would go downstairs and switch off all of the plugs and check the cooker and other appliances. The rituals would ease my anxiety for a short time but when the intrusive thoughts returned the compulsions would worsen.

It was a relentless, exhausting cycle of doom. The more I tried not to think these horrible things the more they would force their way into my mind. It was all consuming like a persistent, threatening monster chipping away at my peace of mind, my happiness.

It was at this time the mild symptoms of UC started although it was another two years before I was officially diagnosed. These early symptoms coupled with the pubescent changes in my body caused me to feel insecure, uncertain and anxious. The warm bubble of childhood had burst and this was unfamiliar territory!

I began experiencing regular bouts of painful diarrhoea. Sometimes it would contain blood and mucus but mostly was just the runs. I would have sporadic days of feeling exhausted with tummy pains and nausea. As it only happened from time to time I tended to ignore it in the hope it would stop. It was not long after my thirteenth birthday that the symptoms developed into something much more concerning.

Becoming a teenager was monumental so my parents arranged a big birthday party to celebrate. All my school friends had been invited and I was so looking forward to it; excitedly planning out all the details of decorations and music with Mum. The big day arrived and I was all keyed up, imagining making a grand entrance looking like a princess, all eyes on me.

It's going to be the best party ever....I thought, fidgeting impatiently as Mum did my hair.

After the longest day imaginable it was time and we got in the car to leave. My heart sank like a brick as I suddenly felt the familiar griping pain in my tummy. *Not tonight please,* I groaned praying it was just butterflies. The pain eased off slightly, but before I had time to feel relief it was replaced with some unsettling waves of nausea.

We got to the venue and it looked amazing with pink and silver balloons, streamers and sparkly banners adorning the walls and tables. The arrival of my friends, who were bouncing around like hyper bunny rabbits took my mind away from how I was feeling. Everyone was dressed up and looked amazing and the party was soon in full swing.

There were groups of girls dancing and other little huddles giggling as they talked about which boys they fancied. Some of the lads were showing off their break dancing moves. When they got bored of this they moved on to having gross competitions to see who could burp the alphabet after drinking a pint of fizzy coke, or who could drink said pint of coke upside down. Everyone was laughing at the boys' antics and I distractedly tried to join in and ignore the persistent waves of sickness.

I didn't even have the energy to dance and was irritated that everyone seemed to be enjoying themselves more than me.

It's supposed to be my night....I thought unhappily.

My parents had put so much effort into making my party special so I tried to make out as though I was having a great time. This was hard work and I felt completely and utterly exhausted, picking tentatively at the buffet in an attempt to disguise how rough I was feeling. The plate of food gave me an excuse to sit down and I gratefully sank into a chair. My appetite was non-existent but I somehow managed to force down a few bread sticks and crisps.

All I really wanted to do was to go home, cuddle up in my cosy bed and sleep. The idea of sleep was so inviting I could have easily curled up on the floor and drifted away. However, there was still an hour of the party left so I reluctantly dragged myself up and went back to being the "life and soul".

Blowing out the candles on my birthday cake proved to be the biggest challenge of the night. The sweet smell of the pink fondant icing almost pushed me over the edge. My mouth went watery as it does immediately before throwing up. Closing my eyes I swallowed back the queasiness and blew the candles out as quickly and as cleanly as I could. My rush meant that I had extinguished them all before my guests finished singing "Happy Birthday" to me! It was either that or like a forest destroyed by a Tsunami, the delicate little sugar roses would have been drowned in vomit!

For weeks I had been anticipating being the centre of attention, a real birthday princess. Unfortunately I was so green, the only princess I resembled was the one from Shrek! It was a blessing that aside from the disco lights and blinding camera flashes, the room was dark! Finally the music stopped and the party ended as in dribs and drabs my friends began to leave.

'Did you have fun Jen?' Mum asked as we filled bin bags with plates of uneaten food and the remnants of exploded party poppers.

'It was amaz.....' I started to reply, as another wave of nausea gripped me fiercely.

This time it won and I promptly vomited all over the floor! My pretty pink shoes now splattered in barf and my belly cramping painfully, ended the night! I was completely naïve to the fact that this was about to become the norm. Life as a teenager had literally begun as it was to continue.

Life on the Loo

After this things quickly deteriorated. I began having multiple days off school with sickness, diarrhoea and general malaise. Mum took me to my GP who wasn't overly concerned and suggested I may have a nervous tummy. Given how severe my anxiety had become over the last year this was plausible enough.

Gradually the intermittent spells of diarrhoea progressed into days of extremely painful diarrhoea which seemed to just pour out of me. It also contained lots of bright red blood and mucus.

I would dread the urgent cramps knowing that a painful hour or more sitting on the toilet was inevitable. Hunched over, staring blindly at the chequered bathroom floor as my poor bottom throbbed and exploded. Sometimes nausea would also take hold and I would be retching into the sink at the same time. I've always been a good multi-tasker!

In all seriousness it seemed as though no matter how much diarrhoea I passed there was still more and more waiting. Finally relief would come and I would gratefully get up off of the uncomfortable toilet only to be gripped with terror when I saw what I had passed. It was as though a violent massacre had taken place; the white porcelain bowl, the unfortunate casualty of this brutal war occurring inside me.

One evening after over an hour of painful diarrhoea, I actually thought my insides had fallen out, it was terrifying!

'Something's really wrong Mum,' I cried showing her the latest horror in the toilet. Hearing her gasp just increased my hysteria and she immediately caught herself.

'Ok, don't panic! I'll make a doctors' appointment first thing tomorrow. She gave me a reassuring hug and added...

We'll get to the bottom of it all'

Despite myself I laughed weakly and realising what she had said, Mum joined me. I got into bed and was sound asleep within minutes, the pain and stress of the relentless diarrhoea had left me exhausted.

I hadn't been to school for over two weeks and the next day was no different. After Mum had finished work we went back to the GPs surgery. Samples of my stool, urine and blood were taken and sent off for analysis. The increasing blood and mucus in my stool seemed to ring alarm bells with the doctor. I was given a referral to a Gastrointestinal (GI) Consultant and we were just advised to wait for that to come through but to return to the surgery immediately if my symptoms worsened.

Over the next month, the diarrhoea continued. It was accompanied by excruciating abdominal pain and nausea. Unable to tolerate food, I was also losing weight quite rapidly. The early GP visits are a bit of a blur, but I remember going back and forth whilst waiting for the hospital referral to come through.

Mum and Dad still had to work during this time so I would spend the days with Nan. Some days I wouldn't be able to go anywhere as I needed to stay close to the toilet to avoid accidents. Becoming increasingly worried about my weight loss and how ill I was looking, Nan would try and tempt me with my favourite foods and treats. She would fry bacon in the hope the smell would make me hungry but I just couldn't stomach it.

'Please try and eat something Jen, I can't see you if you stand sideways.'

She was trying (and failing) to play down how desperately worried she was. I was frightened too. A white face with sunken cheeks and dark circles under the eyes stared back at me every time I looked in a mirror.

I was feeling particularly horrific one afternoon when Mum came to collect me. Spending the majority of the day on the toilet had left me weak, nauseous, lightheaded and strangely breathless. Perched at the top of my Nan's stairs by the toilet door just crying weakly, I barely had the energy to walk out to the car. All I wanted was for the pain to stop for just a moment. Mum almost had to carry me. She helped me into the car seat which wasn't easy as my tail end had become so sore it was painful to sit down. Mum climbed into the car and slammed the door angrily. Fear and frustrated oozed from her.

'Enough is enough; we won't be fobbed off this time!'

By the time we arrived at the GP surgery Mum had calmed slightly. She requested an appointment and firmly explained that we wouldn't be leaving until I had seen a doctor. The receptionist looked at me and ushered us into a quiet separate waiting room with an examination bed on it.

'Have a lie down while you wait dear. You do look poorly,' she said.

Her concerned tone was all it took for the flood gates to open and I cried until there was nothing left. This in itself was exhausting. Ten minutes later the doctor came in and examined me.

'I don't think we can wait for your outpatients' appointment to come through, she said. Let me make a phone call and arrange for you to go into hospital this evening.'

'That's good then isn't it, Mum whispered. We might be closer to finding out what's going on hey!'

I think she half expected me to make a fuss about having to go into hospital. She needn't have worried, there was absolutely no way I was going to get worked up. I had neither the energy nor desire to upset myself and realised, the only emotion I felt was complete and utter relief.

Bums, Tums and Humiliation

As we had been sent to the hospital via my GP, thankfully it wasn't necessary for us to wait for hours in Accident and Emergency. We were directed to go straight to an adult medical ward where they were apparently expecting me. Unfortunately I was no longer at the age where it was deemed appropriate for me to be admitted onto a children's ward.

Mum and I weaved our way through the seemingly endless maze of white corridors until we finally reached our destination. The ward entrance was some flimsy, transparent plastic doors which reminded me of our local supermarkets' freezer section. We pushed them open hesitantly wondering if it was alright to simply enter; however the absence of a buzzer or intercom suggested it was.

I wasn't prepared for the variety of smells which assaulted my nostrils as we walked in. A combination of toilet odours mixed with something remarkably similar to school dinners and a cloying floral air freshener. The mixture confused my senses and my stomach reeled dangerously. It was the food smells which made me feel the most nauseous but before it had time to take hold, a dishevelled looking nurse appeared. She seemed flustered and was carrying a huge tower of towels which were wobbling precariously. Plonking them down on a trolley before they toppled the nurse turned to us.

'Can I help you?'

Mum gave my name and explained that we had come straight from the GPs surgery. The nurse frowned momentarily and then nodded.

'Ah yes, come with me,' she said, leading us to a bed and drawing the curtains around briskly.

'Put the gown on and pop into the bed please,' instructed the nurse pointing to a neatly folded garment on the bed.

The material was light blue splattered with an array of blue diamonds. It was stiff and cold.

20

'It's just so the doctor can examine you easily. Not very fashionable I'm afraid" she added winking conspiratorially.

I didn't really care what I looked like but for some reason hadn't even considered that I would have to change out of my tracksuit. It was slowly dawning on me that I was actually in hospital and I had absolutely no idea what to expect. Once Mum and I had worked out which way the gown went on (back to front with your bum on full display, in case you were wondering) she helped me into the starchy bed.

Beyond tired; I leaned back against the pillows which were surprisingly soft despite looking like concrete boulders. They made a crinkling sound if I moved my head due to the heavy plastic underneath the cotton cases. My bed was situated on a side bay in the ward with four elderly ladies, one of whom kept calling out for the nurse. She sounded so pitiful; I felt really sorry for her. Sorry for her, and scared for myself. It was all so clinical and unfamiliar.

I closed my eyes for a moment but it soon became apparent that sleep wasn't on the agenda. The brusque nurse reappeared with my identification bracelet and went through a form to admit me onto the ward. Over the next few hours' blood, urine and stool tests were taken. Numerous doctors came in to see me, all of whom interrogated me about symptoms, timescales, my periods, my diet and so much more.

It was as though I was a contestant on some strange medical game show with multiple questions being fired at me. Different doctors asking the same things over and over; it was as if they were trying to catch me out somehow. I was getting flustered trying to make sure I gave all the correct information. Mum was helping me as much as she could but there was only so much she could tell them.

Regrettably for me, the next round in the "diagnosis gameshow" Mum couldn't help me with at all. I was scrutinized from head to toe and had to endure a number of physical examinations. One of which (to my absolute horror) involved a doctor putting his finger up my bum! I was utterly mortified. Not only was it humiliating, it was also extremely painful. I sucked in my breath sharply as he slowly inserted a well lubricated finger

'You're doing very well Jennifer. Try to relax.'

His words may have been slightly more soothing had he not been attached to my rectum. Hot tears burned my throat but I choked them back and focused on reading a poster above the sink. It was a very dull poster advertising the correct technique for effective handwashing. However, it provided a much needed momentary distraction!

I was very conscious that if I made a fuss I might appear childish or uncooperative. It was such an intimidating environment even though everyone was friendly they were brisk and pressured. I was given some fluids through a drip in my arm and pain relief as I was quite dehydrated and sore due to the days of excessive diarrhoea and bleeding. The finger up the bum hadn't helped much either!

All Mum and I really wanted were some answers. It was very overwhelming and perplexing with different clinicians coming and going. The final doctor who saw me that evening said that they were still awaiting my test results and further investigations were needed to find out exactly what was making me so unwell. She explained that there were a few possibilities, one being quite probable; something called an Inflammatory Bowel Disease

'I don't have the answers just yet I'm afraid, she said. Tomorrow you will have a procedure, an Endoscopy which will tell us more.'

'An operation?' I murmured looking at Mum nervously.

'No, no it's not surgery; just a simple examination which involves a long thin tube with a camera on the end being inserted into your bottom. It's a quick procedure and the consultant can have a really good look inside of your bowels,' she finished.

I gazed at her in sheer astonishment…a camera into my bottom! Suddenly the finger examination didn't seem so bad after all! The doctors' bleeper went off jerking me back into the room abruptly.

'Sorry, I have to answer this,' she said glancing at it distractedly. The endoscopy will be carried out at some point tomorrow. It's all standard procedure in cases like this, absolutely nothing to worry about.'

With that she gathered up all the paperwork, grabbed her stethoscope and exited the room apparently oblivious to my disbelief and horror.

I wish they would leave my bum alone, I thought before bursting into tears again.

'You're tired Jen, it's been a long day. Things won't seem so bad tomorrow after you have had some sleep,' said Mum.

'I'm not tired! I'm just sick of everything!'

My protests mirrored a petulant toddler trying to fight nap time. I was actually exhausted but the new information had unsettled me. I had so many questions. Would it hurt? What if I needed the loo while they were in the middle of it? How big was this camera they were planning to shove up my arse?

'It sounds so horrible,' I said miserably.

The nurse who had met us on the way in appeared around the curtain. Recognising my distress she put her arm over my shoulder.

'It's all a bit overwhelming I know. Someone will go through everything with you beforehand, so there isn't any point in upsetting yourself' she said kindly.

I could see Mum smiling at the nurse gratefully and realising that she must be feeling worn out too I stopped crying.

'Someone will check in on you later dear, we are just about to have handover,' finished the nurse disappearing as quickly as she had materialised.

Visiting time was over so Mum got herself ready to go home.

'I'll be back tomorrow luvvie, try and rest. I saw a payphone in the corridor on the way in so I will leave some money if you want to call in the morning,' she said kissing me lightly on the head.

She pulled the blankets up and tucked them underneath me snugly. I really didn't want her to go and leave me alone and I could see she was struggling also.

'I am tired now,' I said letting my eyes droop to indicate that it was ok for her to go home. It would have been pointless and unfair to make a commotion.

When I opened my eyes Mum had gone. I wondered what would happen next. There were lots of unfamiliar sounds and sights. One of the old ladies in the bay began crying and I heard her weakly call out.

'Nurse, please come to me.'

It was as though we were somehow cut off from the rest of the world. It was lonely, isolating. I didn't even know if I was permitted to leave my bed area. It sounds silly but I wasn't sure how to behave in this clinical environment. It was like the first day of school but with no instruction, no order.

Sinking wearily against the crinkly pillows I resisted the urge to call a nurse. In all honesty I was slightly intimidated by the stern nurses and didn't want to be a nuisance. Unconsciously I was already conforming to the patient role. It was a role I would need to learn quickly because this was the first of many nights I was to spend alone on a hospital ward

It was an arduous night, I tossed and turned. The plastic under the pillow cases made me hot. I would drift off only to awake abruptly an hour later sweaty and disorientated. My disturbed sleep was exacerbated further by a combination of feeling unwell and anticipation of the endoscopy.

I had to rush to the toilet several times during the night to relieve myself of more agonising diarrhoea. One occasion the pain was so great it caused me to vomit on the floor while sitting on the loo! I was so embarrassed at the mess I had made along with the smelly diarrhoea and didn't want to call for the night shift nurse. She reminded me of a cross head teacher and I had no intention of making her crosser! Instead I shakily cleaned up the vomit with handfuls of tissue and crawled back into bed praying for sleep.

Night turned into day and I was exhausted and anxious. There was lots of hustle and bustle as the daily activities of the ward began. Nurses were milling about carrying bowls of water for patients to have a bedside wash. I was supplied with a bowl of soapy water, towels and toothpaste by a cheery health care assistant.

'Have a little wash and I will get you a fresh gown,' she instructed pulling the curtains around for privacy.

I kept the towel over my chest until she returned with the gown and then quickly washed and put it on. I didn't have a toothbrush; I didn't have anything other than the clothes I arrived in last night. Mum was going to bring in supplies later on. Opting not to bother the nurses I squeezed some gloopy white paste onto my finger and rubbed it all over my teeth instead. It wasn't as effective as a good brush but the zingy mint awoke my senses slightly.

The nurse had made my bed with fresh crisp sheets. I took this as a signal not to get back in even though I desperately wanted to. The only other option was a very uncomfortable upright chair. The varnish on the arms was peeling away and the plastic seat was slightly torn with some of the foam spilling out like guts. It wasn't particularly inviting but I sat on it wondering what was next on the agenda.

Only wearing a hospital gown, and with no dressing gown my legs were icy cold. I pulled the spare blanket off the bed and wrapped it around my bottom half mermaid style. The ward seemed different in the day, the demons of the small hours had disappeared and it wasn't so scary. The little lady from opposite who had cried out a lot during the night now looked happier and gave me a wave from her chair. It seemed the daytime was better for her too.

There was nothing to do other than sit in my chair and watch the world go by. A trolley was pushed in carrying confectionary and newspapers so I used some of the money Mum had left and brought myself a trashy magazine.

I knew that the endoscopy was scheduled for that afternoon and was dreadfully nervous. Desperate for reassurance, I bombarded every nurse that came into the bay with questions about the procedure. To my frustration all they kept saying was that it wouldn't hurt; it would just be a little bit uncomfortable. Why couldn't they understand that my perception of discomfort was something very similar to, if not exactly the same as pain? There was no separating them, and I didn't want to experience either.

My bottom was red raw and literally throbbing from all the toilet trips. It was painful to even sit, so the anticipation of a physical examination made me grimace. The nurses seemed ignorant to my fears. This was a standard procedure to them, performed on many people every day.

I was at an awkward age considered to be on the cusp; too old for the children's ward and too young for the adult ward. I was only thirteen, albeit a mature thirteen, but really I was a frightened bewildered child desperate for reassurance. On this particular ward they were clearly used to dealing with adults who were perhaps more emotionally equipped to cope with invasive medical intervention. It was extremely busy and they didn't have the staff, resources or patience to support an over anxious teenager asking repetitive questions.

I read the magazine from cover to cover and then found myself watching the clock as the procedure time drew closer. It was as though I was waiting to be executed. Melodramatic I know, but that is how terrified I felt! An hour before I was due to go to endoscopy a nurse called Cathy appeared and drew the curtains around my bed. She was brusque and hurried.

'Ok Jennifer, we just need to give you an enema to clear out your bowel before the procedure,' she said.

What is this obsession with putting things up my bum? I thought, making sure it remained as just a thought and kept silent, for fear of seeming silly and immature.

'I don't need that, I've been to the toilet lots,' I pleaded.

Cathy looked at me and sighed wearily as though my reluctance was something she really didn't have time for.

'Come on now love, it needs to be clear so that the doctors can get a proper look at your bowel lining. We don't want to waste anyone's time do we?' she patronized.

I knew she was just doing her job and really didn't want to be difficult but I was scared and helpless. Cathy wasn't saying anything to dispel my fears, quite the opposite in fact.

'It doesn't hurt, it's just a little uncomfortable,' she said.

I could see any protests would be a waste of time. Nurse "uncomfortable not painful" wasn't going to go away. It felt as though she was following a script for difficult patients. Exhausted, I didn't have the strength to make a fuss.

Mum will be here soon, I thought knowing I wouldn't feel quite so lost when she arrived.

Cathy placed a large pad on my bed and then instructed me to lie on my side and draw my knees up to my chest. I clamped my eyes shut as she administered the enema.

'Try and relax, these things are always worse if you tense up,' said Cathy.

Oh shut up you idiot, I thought. *This is hideous!*

It quite amuses me now I am older. I have had countless enemas and endoscopies since this first ordeal and honestly, I don't think twice about it now. Most recently one doctor even laughed once at how quickly I assumed the required position on my side with my knees pulled up. Absolutely no problem with flashing my bottom these days! I can still remember how I felt the first time though and it was very real and awfully embarrassing.

Despite my misconceptions Cathy was right, it didn't hurt, but it was a very weird sensation. My bottom felt full, similar to the feeling of urgently needing a poo. Cathy said I should try and hold it in for at least ten minutes and then I could use the commode (a strange portable toilet with wheels) positioned next to the bed. She was joking right? I only managed about four minutes before the urge to release overcame me.

I flew off the bed and onto the commode. All that separated me from the rest of the ward was the flimsy curtain. So without much privacy I filled this odd toilet with the contents of my bowels, including the occasional explosive fart for good measure! I waited a while before ringing for Cathy to remove the commode. Having been unable to hold the enema in for the instructed ten minutes I was worried she might want to do it again. The whole performance had been mortifying and I certainly didn't want a repeat!

My mum arrived half an hour later and it was such a relief to see her familiar face. She was being deliberately jovial but I knew she was worried. There was little time for us to chat as the porter had arrived to take me for the endoscopy procedure. Mum came with me which was a blessing because her presence really calmed me. The fear of the unknown had started to get the better of me and I was becoming increasingly panicky. We arrived at the department and the porter parked me outside some double doors and went to check me in with the nurses at the reception desk.

'Ello Ducky,' a voice chirped behind me.

It belonged to a rather flamboyant nurse who had her hair piled up on top of her head in a pineapple style and crimson red lipstick covering her very thin lips. I noticed some of it was on her teeth but chose to ignore this. I had enough to worry about. She was carrying a folder of notes.

'Let me just check we have the right patient,' she said examining my identification bracelet.

There was no longer any holding back the tears. I was just a child and it was too much to handle.

'She's a little nervous,' explained Mum.

'Oh there's nowt to worry about, Ducky,' admonished the nurse and before we could say anything else ushered Mum into waiting area and wheeled me into the endoscopy room.

'I'll be right here Jen,' called Mum helpless to do anything other than wait.

As I entered the small examination room there were three people waiting. They were wearing gowns and masks so all I could see were three sets of eyes looking at me. They were accompanied by some intimidating clinical equipment, monitors and machines. A bucket of soapy water sat on the floor. I wondered if this would be used to wash my insides out and began to sob.

They checked all my details again and a lady with pretty eyes above her mask asked me to turn onto my side and raise my knees up. I was approaching hysteria at this point and the lady took my hand. I can remember her face (well the top half anyway) really clearly even now. Perhaps because she was kind to me! The doctor then put some sedation into the needle in my hand explaining that it wouldn't put me completely to sleep but should help me to relax.

Why can't they just knock me out and wake me up afterwards I thought, as I lay trembling.

Unfortunately, sedation isn't as effective if the patient is very stressed or anxious which of course I was. It can have an amnesia type effect meaning that while you are aware of what is happening during the procedure, afterwards the memory of it can

28

be blurry. This wasn't the case with me, probably due to how upset I was. I remember every single detail of my first endoscopy.

The people in the room were talking to each other and I didn't really understand what they were saying. The doctor slowly began to insert the endoscopy tube into my anus and it felt sharp. It didn't hurt particularly but the discomfort and foreign feeling of the tube inside me was still quite horrible. I made such a fuss. Mum said she could hear me crying and shouting at them to stop the entire time she was waiting outside the room. Of course, it was predominantly anticipation and fear that caused my dramatic reaction.

An endoscopy is a routine investigation and I have had endured countless more since, with no sedation and without any problems. My perception of what was going to happen that first time was exaggerated and extreme due to my age. The fear of the unknown is a powerful force! Perhaps if they had explained how the sedation worked or used more child friendly language my nerves may have been manageable. The relief when it was over was palpable. For the endoscopy team as well as me I imagine!

Doctor Doom

Despite it being against protocol, following my endoscopy ordeal I was taken to the children's ward; probably because it was clear that I wasn't adjusting or coping well in the mature environment of the adult ward. There was a much friendlier, warmer vibe and the nurses were really nice and chatty. I was given a side room with a window overlooking a pretty garden, and even better my own ensuite bathroom. No more commodes for me!

I settled in well as Mum had brought me in lots of my own things from home. Visiting hours were more flexible and Mum could even stay overnight with me if I wanted her to.

It was the day after the endoscopy. Although I was glad it was over and was more comfortable in the relaxed ambiance of the children's ward I was still feeling quite poorly. My mum had helped me have a bath and we were both in my room waiting for the consultant to do his rounds. I put my Walkman on (there were no iPods in the nineties) and listened to a mix tape of all my favourite songs trying to take my mind of things.

I had guilelessly decided that now they would know what was wrong with me and would be able to send me home with medication to fix it. My music induced good mood was interrupted when the consultant, Mr Horton who had performed the endoscopy, along with two other doctors and a nurse entered the room. The atmosphere immediately shifted to serious and formal. Mr Horton wasted no time in getting straight to the point.

'Well, young lady, I had a good look around in your large bowel yesterday and found it to be badly inflamed and ulcerated. We will have to wait for the biopsy results for a definite diagnosis but you are suffering with one of two possible conditions; Ulcerative Colitis or Crohn's Disease. Judging by what I saw, I am leaning towards Ulcerative Colitis but as I say the biopsies will give us a clearer picture. These are both chronic diseases but while there is currently no known cure symptoms can be controlled with medication. In your case the ulceration is quite extensive and you are very unwell I'm afraid.'

He stopped talking for a moment and proceeded to examine my tummy. I winced as he pressed down on one side. He turned and muttered something to one of the doctors about writing me up for some pain relief and some other long words I didn't know. He finished examining me and I pulled my nightie back down. Hovering over me he continued his speech.

'At the moment we are quite concerned as the blood tests show that you are very anaemic and because you have had inflammation for some time now, your bowel wall has become quite thin. We are going to give you a blood transfusion and start you on some steroids and an anti-inflammatory drug called Mesalazine. I have to warn you that there is a risk of your bowel perforating. We will be monitoring you closely and if things deteriorate we will need to act immediately. The next forty eight hours are crucial with regards to getting things back to a manageable level.'

I felt as though I had been slapped across the face. This wasn't what I had anticipated at all. So much for being packed off home with some medicine. All of a sudden I needed blood, my bowel could perforate and the next forty eight hours were critical. That was the sort of thing they said in TV medical dramas when they someone was about to die!!

Obviously that wasn't the context in which it was meant but in my anxious state that was how I interpreted it and I was stunned and scared. Looking over at Mum for reassurance, my heart sank further when I saw how visibly upset she was. Nothing is more frightening to a child than seeing fear in your parents' eyes.

'How has it got to such a serious stage, said Mum. Surely something should have been done sooner, before it got this bad.'

To my disbelief, Mr Horton rolled his eyes.

'What on earth do you mean? We are doing everything possible!'

His annoyance was clear and painfully uncomfortable. Poor Mum was so distressed and the unsympathetic consultants' blunt response was too much. I had been having symptoms for months. It had taken numerous GP visits and many instances of feeling fobbed off before we were finally getting some answers; answers which were not being given with much tact or empathy. The fact I was so dangerously unwell was a shock to us both and we were understandably upset.

I began to cry. Mr Horton softened slightly and explained that a specialist nurse would come and talk us through everything and answer any questions we had. With a brisk 'good evening' he left us to process the information.

Mum went out into the corridor for a moment. The nurse stayed in the room with me and was so lovely. I hadn't noticed before but she was holding my hand.

'They don't have much of a bedside manner these doctors. Try not to get worked up Jennifer. Let me go and get you some pain relief and we will see if we can get you a little more comfortable; how does that sound?' she asked plumping up my pillows.

Her presence was comforting and I didn't really want her to leave but I agreed, feebly sinking back on the bed. I could hear Mum sobbing outside. I knew she was feeling exhausted and humiliated by Mr Hortons' snappy unsympathetic manner. I had never seen or heard my mum cry before, she was always so strong. This scared me more than anything.

Thankfully and at exactly the right moment my Auntie and Uncle arrived for a visit. Auntie Sam came in to me carrying her daughter Lucy who was nearly a year old. My Uncle had stayed outside with Mum and I could hear him trying to console her and find out what was happening. I took one look at Sam and began to cry again.

'I don't want to die'.

'Oh Jen, you're not going to die!'

Sam put Lucy down on the bed next to me and gave me a cuddle. Somehow saying my fear out loud had made it slightly less scary. Sam was really calming and so certain that everything would be ok that I started to feel a little better. It was exactly what I had needed at that moment. Sometimes, even if it might not be true it just helps to hear that everything is going to be alright.

Mum and Uncle Jack came back in the room and the tension had lifted a little. The nice nurse had delivered tea and biscuits on a tray for my visitors. I would have loved a drink but was still nil by mouth and unable to partake. It was all a happy distraction though.

Lucy began crawling around on the bed. She was so cute; it was nice to have something else to focus on. Then she made her way up towards my feet and promptly bit my big toe! We all burst out laughing which startled her for a moment but then she joined in with a toothy grin loving the attention. I think Mum and I were laughing a little too hysterically. More of a tension release than genuine laughter I suppose.

As I'm writing this I'm aware that I come across as a real wimp or a drama queen. I do cringe when I reflect on some of my reactions during the early days of diagnosis. However, I also know I have a tendency to be quite hard on myself. If I were a bystander watching someone going through the ordeals I faced I would view it differently. I would think they were brave and that they had every right to feel afraid and overwhelmed.

I was a young teenager being given life changing, upsetting news in a clinical and if I'm honest, at times, unfeeling manner. I didn't possess the maturity or life skills to process such information calmly and rationally. The fact that I suffered with anxiety just magnified every emotion tenfold. In many ways I grew up on the day I received my diagnosis. I knew that I never, ever wanted to see my mum so distraught again, that was unbearable. Although I didn't realise at the time I possessed a great deal of strength and resilience. This would be something I would draw on this more and more in order to fiercely protect those I loved from feeling my pain.

Despite having the fear of god put into me, the next two days were uneventful in terms of bowel perforation, septicaemia and emergency surgery. The initial night of my diagnosis I was so paranoid my bowel was going to perforate and that I was going to die I was too frightened to sleep. I honestly believed I wouldn't wake up again and every time I began to snooze, the anxiety would startle me back into consciousness. Mum stayed with me that night on a little sofa bed which was a huge comfort although she didn't get much sleep either!

My treatment began immediately and I was given Prednisolone (Steroids) and Mesalizine. These were administered through my IVinitially in order to get them absorbed into my system quickly. I loathed it when the nurses injected the Steroids through the needle in my hand twice a day. Every single time, as soon as the drug hit my veins my bottom would itch and burn so violently, I would almost fly off the bed! I'm sure they thought I was exaggerating as the nurses said they had never seen such a reaction before. This spiteful side effect continued until a few days later when I was finally able to take my medication orally. Another ordeal survived and chalked up to experience!

I was also given three pints of blood. It was strange to see this deep claret flow from a bag down a tube into my hand. I would watch it hypnotised; someone else's blood, drip, drip, drip. Nan told me the blood had been donated by an Irish person and that I would probably start talking with an Irish accent. I knew it wasn't true but I played along as it made everyone laugh. She chuckled about it for years afterwards.

I had to go back to using the uncomfortable commode despite having the en-suite as the nurses needed to monitor my stool.

'Why do I have to keep showing people my poo?' I moaned to Mum.

I was however, slowly becoming immune to the characteristic embarrassment of an IBD. Poo, wee, wind, loose stool, anus and bloody mucus were all fast becoming a part of my daily vocabulary. The results of the biopsies taken had confirmed that I had UC and not Crohn's so the doctors now knew exactly what they were treating.

The medication was quickly taking effect. Within five days all of my symptoms were easing. It was amazing and made it difficult to believe I had been so unwell. After a week I was back to what was considered "normal" bowel movements and was feeling so much better. The medical team were pleased with my progress and then came the happy news I had been waiting for. After two weeks in hospital I was ready to go home.

Before my discharge a nurse called Sue came down to see Mum and I. Sue was a Specialist Gastroenterology Nurse and knew everything there was to know about IBD. It was all so new to us and a lot to absorb. Sue gave us some literature and leaflets to read and explained we could ring her directly if we had any questions or concerns which was very reassuring. Finally after learning my medication regime and arranging an outpatient's appointment for six weeks' time I was free to go! I practically danced out of that ward. I was better (or so I thought) and could not wait to get home and put this awful experience behind me!

Things went well for a while. I returned to school and was a bit of a celebrity after my stay in hospital. All of my friends wanted to hear my story, to them it was dramatic and exciting and I enjoyed being the centre of attention. Although I did leave out some of the more embarrassing details! It was simpler to say that I had ulcers in my tummy and mention nothing of explosive diarrhoea and cameras up my bum.

Physically, I was feeling really well and had more energy than I had had in a long time. The medication I was prescribed, especially the steroids came with quite a long list of possible side effects. They can impact on emotions, promoting feelings of wellbeing along with unpredictable mood swings. I had moments of euphoria and could be quite excitable alternating with times of feeling low and being quite tearful. This may not have been due to the medication however; it could have been a side effect of raging adolescent hormones.

In my happy moments I would be excited about the future. It was lovely to be back with my school friends and I was looking forward to planning weekends together doing fun things like shopping or trips to the cinema and the bowling alley. I had been given a new lease of life which wasn't to be taken for granted after feeling poorly for so long. As the symptoms had disappeared I genuinely believed that the UC had been cured.

Another common side effect of steroids is an increase in appetite. I was taking a high dose and my appetite was beyond belief! I was constantly ravenous and nothing would fill me up or satisfy the hunger pangs. In the morning I would devour a full cooked breakfast only to want a sandwich or crisps and chocolate twenty minutes later. This would continue all day and sometimes I would wake during the night and lie in bed craving cheese and biscuits and jam doughnuts.

Mum was so relieved that I was interested in food again that I could pretty much have anything I wanted. Safe to say I wasn't very sensible with my diet choices. All I wanted was stodge and tasty calorie laden treats, the healthier options held no appeal whatsoever. It would probably be difficult for most people to adhere to a healthy diet in the midst of such a massive appetite increase.

My weight began to creep up, which wasn't a problem initially. I had been very slim before diagnosis and during my initial flare up of UC had lost over a stone. As time went on however I did gain too much weight. This just chipped away at my confidence and self-image more and more. I already felt so different to my peers and excessive weight gain did nothing to help the situation.

The day of my outpatients' appointment arrived. Mum took the afternoon off work and we arrived at the hospital that I had been ecstatic to leave six weeks earlier. The waiting room was a sea of blue chairs most of which were occupied but we found a couple empty and sat down.

A nurse took me to be weighed and then asked me to go back to the waiting room. I was starting to get bored and fidgety and picked up a magazine. I couldn't concentrate; I just wanted to get this over with so I could go back to school and meet my friends. An hour later my name was called and I was ushered into one of the small consulting rooms. I trotted in happily, not expecting anything other than a quick chat. After all I was feeling so much better.

The doctor asked me to get up on the examination couch and he laid a hand on my tummy and listened with his stethoscope. Seemingly satisfied he instructed me to take a seat in the chair and asked me how I had been feeling or if there had been any problems since my discharge to which I relied no and that I was feeling great.

What he said next completely threw me and I have never forgotten how it made me feel.

'I see the steroids have caused your face to fatten considerably.'

It is unfortunate that a medical professional failed to see how potentially damaging such a blasé' remark could be. Especially when directed at a sensitive and already self-conscious young woman. I doubt that particular doctor would remember me now, much less remember ever making that comment. From his perspective it was simply a medical observation.

There are so many occasions during my years of illness when I have felt like a case of medical interest; a problem which needs solving, rather than a person with feelings and needs. This particular lack of sensitivity, along with many others did have a lasting effect on me. The doctor was correct; I had a big round face. For years afterwards this was all I would see when I looked in the mirror.

While I genuinely appreciate that doctors and nurses have massive workloads and tremendous stresses; it must be recognised that one of the most powerful tools or skill sets needed in this profession is empathy and understanding. Medications and treatments are wonderful and I was fortunate enough to have access to what I needed. I believe they would have been a more effective if they had been used alongside compassion and sensitivity.

I didn't answer or acknowledge what the doctor said and he briskly moved on deciding that things were progressing in the right direction. He then explained that it was time to begin reducing the steroids. On the whole, physically everything was looking positive and the medication had so far produced the desired effect. I was no longer losing blood on opening my bowels and the diarrhoea was a thing of the past.

Steroids are incredibly effective, however they can cause many additional health issues if used long term. They also can't be stopped suddenly, so I was instructed how to safely wean myself off them by dropping the dose slightly every week. The hoped outcome would be that I would get to as low a dose as possible or ultimately off them altogether without the UC "flaring up" and the symptoms returning. The undesirable side effects of the steroids were enough to make me want to try and manage without them. I was gaining weight, had mood swings and now, courtesy of "Doctor Insensitive" I had a fat moon face

37

to worry about! It felt exciting to try and reduce the medication, it was a new challenge. A final step back to normality, or so I thought.

Steroids - Dancing with the Devil

Anyone suffering from an IBD and being treated with steroids will know that the process of reducing them isn't a straightforward one. The next six months of my life was a cycle of lowering the dose (I would usually get down to around ten mg) only to have the debilitating symptoms of the disease return with a vengeance. My GP would then advise me to increase the dose again in order to get things back under control.

While long term steroid use can be damaging, the symptoms and risks posed by the UC outweighed this and were considered the priority. I put a lot of pressure on myself during this time, unable to grasp that it was out of my control. When I got the dosage down I would be on the phone to family and friends to tell them. It almost felt as though it was a massive personal achievement. So, obviously it was quite a blow to me every time the dosage had to be increased. I genuinely believed that I had failed. I almost felt ashamed that I was unable to get control over this embarrassing disease.

The summer holidays arrived. Due to the recurrent "flare ups" of UC, I had missed so much of the school year that breaking up for the summer didn't really make much difference to me. Still, we had a big family holiday to Dorset planned and I was really excited about that. There were quite a few of us going together including two sets of aunties and uncles, my cousins and Nan.

We had all been looking forward to it for ages and had loads of fun activities planned. The weather was perfect, hot and sunny and it was fun living in a caravan and having BBQs in the evenings.

One afternoon we went for a walk to a small harbour on the outskirts of the caravan park. I was having a great time with my cousins. We were crabbing and our buckets were overflowing with clawed critters.

A big black dog was entertaining us by jumping off the small pier into the sea. Our laughing seemed to attract him; he would dance around our feet shaking ice cold water over us before leaping back into the sea.

Just as I was really enjoying myself, it hit me. The dreaded sensation indicating that I needed to find a toilet very urgently. That is how it would happen, suddenly and without warning. I would literally feel as though I was going to mess myself. It was awful. There were no public toilets nearby so the only option was to run back to the caravan and hope for the best. Nan said she was tired of the beach and would come with me.

It wasn't actually that far but with every tentative step and clench of my buttocks it felt like miles. My thirteen year old legs couldn't run fast enough and I have no idea how I held it in, trying desperately not to think about it and to focus on other things. It was at the point of painful and all I could think was every step was a step closer to relief.

Nan was chatting away in an attempt to distract me. I loved her for trying but couldn't speak. Eventually we reached our caravan. Words cannot describe how glorious it was to sit down on the toilet and release. The steroids had been reduced down to quite a low dose so this episode was the result of yet another nasty flare up. Days of painful diarrhoea and sickness followed and to my bitter disappointment the family holiday was cut short. Inevitably the steroids had to be put back up to a higher dose again.

I resented this bloody disease so much, it ruined everything! This was the one of many spiteful flare ups I had suffered on reducing the steroids. It seemed a higher dose was the only way to control the disease and it was all a horrible nightmare.

All in the Mind

This pattern continued over the next six months. I was gaining weight at quite a rate even though Mum and I were trying to be mindful of my diet. I wasn't happy with the way things were going but it was out of my control. The UC was flaring up regularly; even the higher doses of steroids were struggling to keep it in remission.

Aside from the occasional day I was well enough to attend school, the majority of my time was spent with Nan. One day, when I was feeling particularly sorry for myself she said we were going on a mystery tour. We hopped on a bus and it was very exciting as I had no idea what was planned or where we were headed. After twenty minutes we arrived at our destination which was Coventry Cathedral.

We spent the afternoon exploring and learning about the history of this beautiful landmark. Although I wasn't well, I had a great time! We stopped to have tea and cake in a little café and Nan said that it was important that I learnt something new every day; even the days I wasn't in school.

As we were leaving we passed a bedraggled man outside of the cathedral ferreting through a dustbin. He had fingerless gloves on but his exposed skin was a blistering, angry puce. His hunched shoulders made him appear small and sad.

Telling me to wait, Nan nipped back into the café. She reappeared a few minutes later with a hot drink and a cake. Without uttering a word she handed the snacks to the man along with her gloves and scarf. It was a simple gesture of kindness and she was discreet enough not to draw attention to the chap or embarrass him in any way. The man gratefully squeezed her arm and the look of gratitude in his lonely eyes has never left me. I learnt so much that day and knew that I wanted to be just like this kind beautiful woman.

The novelty of my situation had worn off and I was no longer a celebrity at school. My friends were getting on with their own lives. They felt bad for me and wanted me to get better but it was a case of out of sight, out of mind due to my regular absences. I was missing out academically, socially and slowly becoming quite isolated.

I felt poles apart from my peers particularly the boys. Having a boyfriend wasn't high on my list of priorities. There was enough to worry about and quite honestly it was the last thing on my mind. I certainly didn't want to discuss my bowel disease with teenage lads. That would have been far too embarrassing! My close girlfriends would gossip about boys they fancied, who they had snogged. I just couldn't imagine ever feeling comfortable enough to even talk to a boy let alone anything else.

Overtime, avoiding school and social interactions became the norm. Sometimes it was due to feeling physically unwell, other times it was the result of anxiety and the fact I felt so alienated, so different.

After school, large groups of kids would go to the local park where experimenting with alcohol, drugs and cigarettes was a common pastime. The thought of going along filled me with absolute dread yet at the same time I would feel envious.

They would come into school, full of tales of the previous night's antics. Who had got with who, who had been the most drunk and not able to walk. To be involved in these shenanigans was to be a member of the "in crowd". My lack of desire to join in made me feel even more of a freak.

I would spend time with Amy on my "good days" but these were few and far between and the gap between us seemed to widen as I edged further away. In the evenings after school I just wanted to be at home with my family. This was where I felt secure; shutting the world out was a relief. Ninety percent of the time I didn't have a choice anyway as I needed to be close to the toilet.

I know now that I really wasn't missing out on much by hanging around with the rebellious kids at school. At the time I felt massively abnormal, excluded and terribly insecure. I wish I could go back to give that lost teenage girl a hug and let her know that she didn't need to worry about things so much. Some of the insecurities I experienced were just part of the normal transition from childhood to adulthood. It's just they were amplified due to my illness, the medication and social isolation.

I was learning to live with the symptoms of a 'flare up.' As long as the steroids were maintained at a high dose the UC was reasonably controlled. However, it was due to the steroids that everything was about to be turned upside down.

I was awoken from my sleep one night with a vicious pain in the middle of upper abdomen just under my rib cage. It radiated all the way through to my back and took my breath away. My mum heard me crying and came to see what was wrong. I took some paracetamol and Mum climbed into bed next to me. After an hour or so the pain began to ease and I drifted back off to sleep. I felt better the following morning and got ready for school as usual.

'Maybe you had a touch of heartburn,' Mum speculated.

We decided it wasn't worth fretting about unless the pain returned or I had any other new symptoms. Well, a few days later the pain did return, with a vengeance! Mum wasted no time is getting me a doctors' appointment. I was becoming a regular at the surgery; even the receptionist knew my first name without looking at her computer.

We sat in the stuffy waiting room and I rested my head on Mums' shoulder. Two little girls were arguing over a toy in the children's area and I tried to focus on who would win the battle rather than the nasty pain. I never did find out as my name rang out over the tannoy system.

The GP sent me straight back to the hospital. The sudden onset of pain was a concern so I was admitted to have some tests. I really resented being back in the dreary, sterile hospital. The pain would come and go and when it alleviated again I tried to convince the doctors to let me go home.

My protests fell on deaf ears and I was placed on the adult GI ward again. I didn't much like that either but there were no available beds on the more cheerful adolescent ward I had stayed on previously. This also meant that Mum couldn't stay with me. I just felt safer with her there but I knew there was no point making a fuss. The pain had subsided slightly so I told myself that I would probably only have to stay one night. I could handle that.

As the ward was quietening down for the night, the pain returned and it was much worse than before. I had never experienced pain like it and pray that I never do again. This time it was constant, there was absolutely no let up. I tried sitting up, lying down, walking around but no position would provide relief. It was always in exactly the same place, just under my ribs going across like a band and through to my back.

I rang my bell and told one of the nurses who said she would bleep the on call doctor. I was so thankful when the doctor appeared a couple of hours later. After a brief examination the lady doctor looked at my notes. She was displaying a slightly baffled expression.

'We were concerned about a condition called pancreatitis which can sometimes happen when taking steroids but your blood tests showed no indication of this.'

'Please do something; it really hurts' I cried.

The doctor was nice and sympathetic but said that as the blood tests had returned negative the pain was probably just stress related. She tentatively explained that she was going to arrange for a counsellor to come and talk to me about how I was feeling. In the meantime she would ask the nurses to treat me for trapped wind. I desperately tried to impress upon her just how severe and real the pain was but only got the repeated response that the test results indicated otherwise. What was to follow was the worst twenty four hours of my life.

I know that all the nurses and doctors believed that the pain was psychosomatic. That I was just a dramatic teenager who was struggling to come to terms with the diagnosis of UC. However, there was absolutely no doubt in my mind, this agony was real, and it was steadily getting worse! I kept ringing my nurse call bell, literally begging for help whilst writhing around on the bed. This was a pointless operation; it was becoming clear that no one was hearing me. One nurse even told me off for crying so loudly!

'You really need to calm down dear, you are disturbing the other patients,' she tutted straightening my tangled bedsheets and tucking them firmly underneath me.

I can still picture her irritated face and I can say without remorse that I wanted to punch it! It was a long, lonely and horrible night. Every minute was sixty seconds of torture without respite. The morning eventually came and I prayed it would bring with it some form of relief. Unfortunately this was not to be!

During the doctors rounds it was reiterated that I was likely suffering from stress related pain although my blood tests were to be repeated to double check. Nothing stronger than paracetamol was given to me at any time during this ordeal.

A nurse came and said that my mum had telephoned to see how I was today and to let me know she would visit after work. *They must have told her that I was ok*, I thought in horror. If she had any idea of the state I was in she would have been by me side immediately; making sure some action was taken to find out what was going on. I begged them to phone her back. I had been awake for hours in so much pain and just wanted my mum.

'She will be in to visit you after work Jennifer,' the nurse echoed.

By now I was really beginning to feel frightened. I knew instinctively that I was experiencing a dangerous level of pain and that something was seriously wrong. Although the blood tests hadn't confirmed anything, the reality was I was extremely unwell. I was in hospital which is often referred to as the "best place" for someone who is ill. It sure didn't feel that way to me!

The day continued as the night had. There was simply no relief from the horrendous agony. I was crying and sobbing and no one seemed to be listening to me; it was so cruel. A lady visiting someone in the bed opposite me was so concerned at my distress that she actually went to speak to the nurses on my behalf. Sadly it was to no avail as they couldn't discuss my care with her due to confidentiality. The lady came and sat on my bed with me and just held me. She was so genuinely kind and although it didn't take the pain away it was a real comfort. I never knew her name but have never forgotten the compassion she showed me on that awful day.

After she left I curled up into a ball and wept, wondering if I was dying. I stayed like this until Mum and Nan arrived to visit me. My concept of time was distorted but Mum had finished work so it must have been early evening. Well she took one look at me and completely lost it! Her face was ashen and

45

she was trembling with of fear and rage. I could hear her shouting at the nurses.

'Why didn't someone bloody call me, look at the state of her, she isn't putting this on you know!'

Nan just sat by my bed holding my hand and crying quietly. I didn't have the strength to tell her not to get upset. A doctor appeared and explained to my mum that they had decided to take me for a scan. There was a possibility, albeit an unusual one that I did have pancreatitis despite it not showing on my original blood tests.

By this stage the pain was starting to make me a little delirious. Hardly surprising as it had been excruciating and constant for almost twenty four hours. I don't remember going in to the scan room but I do recall being violently sick afterwards. I have no recollection of returning to the ward either but suddenly I was there. The curtains were drawn around my bed and Mum was beside me lovingly stroking my hair. I could hear people talking somewhere nearby and an urgent voice said,

'Its' acute pancreatitis, can we get her some appropriate analgesia and anti-emetics written up immediately please!'

A nurse gave me an injection of morphine in my bottom. They could have stuck needles into me anywhere and I wouldn't have cared.

'Wriggle your toes for me Jenny,' instructed the nurse as she plunged the long overdue pain medication into me.

The relief I felt was almost instantaneous. It was wonderful. Blissful, heavenly respite! I was utterly exhausted and easing the pain caused me to fall asleep almost immediately. I was awoken some time later when a doctor fitted me with a special pump that would release regular doses of morphine.

Nan had gone home but Mum was still with me. She was so upset that I had been left in such agony that she had refused to leave my side. Despite it being against protocol no one dared to argue with her. The next twenty four hours were worlds apart from the last. I drifted in and out of consciousness, so grateful for the sweet oblivion after hours of horrendous pain!

When I reflect on how my care and treatment was managed, the misdiagnosis of pancreatitis was and still is the most difficult to accept. Pancreatitis is an agonisingly spiteful condition. It causes pain which could easily bring a grown man to his knees. I was effectively a child being told that this torturous misery was all in my head. This coupled with the failure to contact my mum was simply unforgivable.

When I finally received the correct diagnosis and appropriate treatment began there was a definite shift in the attitude of the staff towards me. There was never an apology, it was simply stated that it was rare and unfortunate that the pancreatitis failed to show up on the blood test.

Mum and I have often spoken of how we probably should have placed an official complaint. It wouldn't have changed anything for me; there was no taking the awful experience away. It had happened; it was over and I was being treated accordingly. Honestly, the utter relief that the pain had finally ceased left me with no desire to make a fuss.

Hospital patients are vulnerable and many who stay in for lengthy periods can feel they lose not only their identity but the ability to control what happens to them. It is scary to feel so powerless. Granted, it can take time and numerous tests to reach the correct diagnosis and appropriate treatment plan. Unfortunately tests are not infallible and mistakes do get made. So we rely on those qualified to listen to us and help us through.

A patient crying in agony should most certainly *never* be overlooked, chastised or assumed mentally ill! I was angry for quite a long time afterwards; occasionally I still feel a sense of disbelief that I wasn't listened too and left to suffer such agony. Twenty four hours of pain may not seem like such a long time; however the level of pain that comes with pancreatitis meant that every minute felt like an hour.

I pray that it isn't something that happens often but sadly I imagine there are countless patients who have felt ignored and in some way let down. The doctors treating me did appear to be genuinely shocked when a diagnosis of pancreatitis was finally ascertained.

It would have been extremely satisfying to say to the nurse who scolded me for crying....

'I bloody well told you I was in pain!!!'

Between the Devil and the Deep Blue Sea

It was now vital that I reduced and came off the steroids as quickly as possible. They had caused the pancreatitis and were therefore no longer a viable or safe treatment option for me. I had to have my blood sugar checked by the nurses twice a day in case the pancreatitis was causing any abnormalities there.

The morphine pump was doing its job so thankfully I was pain free. My appetite had returned now the pain had settled. However to help my pancreas to recover I wasn't allowed to eat. Instead a gastric tube was fitted to supply me with the nutrition I required. This was crap because all I could think about was food. Visiting times I would pester my mum asking her to tell me in detail everything she had eaten that day.

'I've only had a cheese and pickle sandwich Jen,' she said laughing at the look of pure longing on my face.

It sounded like a banquet to me. I could picture it, god I could almost taste it!

A dietician came to see me on the ward. She explained that when I eventually began eating again I would have to stick to a low fat diet for a few months while my pancreas recovered from the inflammation. I was given a list of the foods I would be allowed to safely eat. To give myself something to occupy my time I used the list to prepare menu plans ready for the day I could eat again. This was both very satisfying and torturous at the same time.

I found myself salivating at the thought of vegetable soup (I don't even like vegetable soup) and craving dry baked potatoes with salad while meticulously planning out my future meals. When denied regular sustenance, foods which would usually hold no appeal quickly become awfully desirable.

Being completely nil by mouth meant that I wasn't permitted to drink either, I was being kept hydrated via a drip. This didn't prevent me from being unbelievably thirsty which was even harder to cope with than the hunger pangs. I found myself daydreaming about long cool glasses of sweet lemonade. At breakfast time I would watch enviously as the other patients in my bay casually sipped refreshing cups of tea.

The lady opposite me had a bottle of orange cordial on her bedside table. It was really annoying because she never seemed to drink any of it and it just sat there callously taunting my dry mouth. My desperation was so great that I actually considered creeping over and pinching some in the middle of the night. It took a lot of restraint to make do with swilling tap water around my mouth instead!

The nurses did take pity on me and allowed the occasional ice cube to suck. This was absolute heaven! I was prescribed a special mouthwash to treat some nasty ulcers and sores on my gums too. It tasted just like aniseed and even though I had to spit it out the sensation of something other than ice in my mouth made my taste buds dance. I even looked forward to brushing my teeth! It is odd to think such a routine activity helped to keep me sane!

Aside from the bouts of diarrhoea which inevitably worsened as the doctors reduced my steroid dosage, I wasn't feeling too awful. I had grown accustomed to living with the symptoms of UC having endured them for quite some time now. The painful cramps, tiredness and diarrhoea were the norm for me. At home I had things to entertain me and take my mind off it all. This wasn't so easy to do in the hospital and I was becoming increasingly bored. At least when I had been placed on the children's ward there were more age appropriate puzzles, books and games to help fill the time. Here there wasn't nearly so much on offer.

There was one television set in the day room for all of the patients to share. This was monopolised by a rather grumpy man who got up at six every morning and would position himself firmly in front of it. There he would remain for the rest of the day watching a constant stream of boring gardening and news programs. If you dared to change the channel then he would make his displeasure obvious creating a very uncomfortable atmosphere! His resolve to let no one interfere with his daily viewing was admirable to say the least. It wasn't worth the hassle so I mostly kept away and stayed by my bed.

To keep busy I worked on a cute cross stitch of a fluffy mother cat and kittens snuggled together by a cosy glowing fire, read lots of books and magazines but mostly, I just watched people.

A young woman, Sarah was admitted to my bay. She was in her early twenties and had a learning disability which meant she couldn't communicate easily. She was accompanied by her fiercely protective mother who rarely left her side. When I first saw Sarah I thought she was pregnant, her belly was so swollen and round. It turned out the poor girl was severely constipated so the swelling was not the result of a baby but an ample amount of impacted poo!

It was quite interesting listening to other patients' stories. It made me feel less alone somehow. I wasn't being deliberately nosy, I was just so bored and although the medical team would always draw the curtains around a patients' bed during a consultation the only privacy this ensured was visual. Hearing what was being discussed couldn't really be avoided.

I heard the doctors explaining to Sarah and her mother that they would try to clear her blocked bowels using an enema and some laxatives. Over the next few hours, Sarah spent most of her time filling bed pan after bed pan. No sooner had the nurses taken away one overflowing cowboy hat another would be needed immediately. I empathised greatly knowing just how exhausting spending hours on the toilet can be!

The smell was extremely strong and although copious amounts of lemon air freshener was sprayed in a futile attempt to mask it, eventually it became too much and our entire bay relocated to the day room. Much to the annoyance of grumpy television man I hasten to add!

I couldn't believe my eyes when I saw Sarah later on. Her previously rotund abdomen was now completely flat. The difference was astounding; she must have been so awfully uncomfortable beforehand!

Sarah only stayed in for one night and seemed to find the whole experience quite bewildering. This was especially evident after her mum had gone home that evening. She would come and sit next to me, holding my hand or playing with my hair. The nurses would come and steer her back to her own bed but she always wandered back. We didn't talk or interact particularly but the company and human contact was nice.

The days were very long in hospital; especially without the luxury of meals or television to help break up the time. I had been in for a month and it felt like a lifetime. Despite lots of people milling about and the daily hustle and bustle of the ward it was a lonely and depressing experience.

The following day Sarah was discharged and within an hour another young girl took her bed. Laura was the same age as me, had Crohn's Disease and was a regular patient on Ward Five. Her parents would chat a little to Mum which was nice as they understood what we were going through.

So much of Laura's bowel had become diseased; she had over time endured multiple operations to remove the affected areas. She was fed through a tube and would be for the rest of her life. Her body struggled to absorb nutrients and she was painfully thin. Her gaunt face gave her the appearance of a frail old lady rather than the vibrant young woman she should have been.

Four days after she came onto the ward Laura was moved to intensive care and that was the last we saw of her and her parents. The outlook for this girl was extremely bleak and her situation emphasises the severity of IBD and how potentially life threatening it can be. Mum didn't tell me any of this until I was much older. I'm grateful as it would have really frightened me, although I think I was aware on some level that Laura was extremely ill.

Although some days were extremely hard and there were awful low points, it wasn't all doom and gloom. It was my fifth week on the ward. I was devouring a well-worn copy of my favourite Judy Blume book to distract me from the cruelty of breakfast exclusion. My reading was interrupted when a porter delivered a lady to the empty bed next to mine. I smiled politely at her and went to continue with my book planning to quietly suss her out as she settled in.

Everyone is so different, some patients are glad to make conversation and exchange pleasantries and others prefer to keep to themselves. It is such an odd situation, strangers thrown together, sitting around in nightclothes. It is like being forced to attend a very awkward and dull slumber party.

'Hiya neighbour; how long you been stuck in here for then?' the lady said flashing me an infectious smile.

She was so friendly and open; I relaxed in her company immediately. She instinctively seemed to know when I wanted to be alone and when I wanted to chat. I could read her emotions easily too. We would alternate between sitting in a companionable silence and chatting animatedly for hours, sharing our fears and hospital horror stories.

Like me, Gemma suffered from UC and had done for six years; it was wonderful to talk to someone who really understood how awful it could be. She was on quite a cocktail of medication including steroids which had unfortunately resulted in the development of additional health problems.

Gemma found it difficult to exercise due to painful and inflamed joints (a common occurrence in sufferers of UC). This coupled with the long term steroid treatment required to control the UC had caused her to become very overweight. Gemma confided in me that she needed to have surgery to treat her UC but was deemed too high a risk because of her weight.

'I lost two stone before this flare up ya know. Now it's all gonna go back on cus of the blasted steroids,' she wailed her eyes swimming with tears.

Despite her frustration it wasn't often you would see her cry. She had a lot to deal with but always tried to remain upbeat and positive. On finding something funny Gemma's pretty round face would light up and her raucous laughter would instantly lift the miserable atmosphere on the ward.

She was lovely to me, I think she sensed that I felt a little bit lost and homesick, especially when visiting hours were over and my parents went home. Before my illness I had only ever spent the odd night away from home and although I was fast adapting to hospital life it was still tough.

On days when the symptoms of diarrhoea were particularly bad the nurses would bring commodes to beside the bed to save us running to and from the toilets every ten minutes. Sometimes Gemma and I would find ourselves sitting on those awful commodes at the same time with nothing but a flimsy curtain separating us. We would get the giggles and end up laughing hysterically, especially if one of us let out an accidental fart!

Our laughter and silliness went a long way to making some of the embarrassing moments slightly less mortifying. I affectionately nicknamed Gemma my "fartner in crime" which made her laugh like a drain. The time we spent together on the ward was certainly the most tolerable I experienced and I was selfishly disappointed when Gemma was well enough to go home. Even though she was my friend I secretly resented that she was free to go when I had to stay. Just before she left the ward we exchanged addresses and she gave me a hug squeezing me tightly.

'Keep smiling kiddo,' she said waving as she walked out to freedom.

For a few years afterwards we sent each other a card at Christmas but eventually this fizzled out and we sadly lost touch. I know her journey with UC was complicated and often painful. I look back on our time as bed buddies with a smile. She didn't know it but she helped a scared young girl through some very difficult days on that miserable hospital ward. Who knows, maybe what we shared helped her as well!

I had now been on Ward Five for six long weeks. We had hit a wall with my treatment and I was proving to be a complicated case for the medical team. Every single time the steroids were reduced to a lower dose the UC would flare up ferociously and I could see my chances of getting home were slipping further away.

Some days I would be running to the toilet every twenty minutes, at times sitting there for over an hour feeling utterly drained as the diarrhoea just poured out. I considered taking a book in with me but as I was usually doubled over it would have been impossible to concentrate. It was miserable.

I was anaemic and my bowel wall was becoming dangerously thin again putting me at risk of a perforation. It seemed I had reverted all the way back to exactly as I was at my initial diagnosis and it was both worrying and frustrating. The doctors and nurses kept saying that I was "between the devil and the deep blue sea." I needed the steroids to control the UC but because of the pancreatitis they weren't a sustainable treatment option.

I was stuck and it was becoming increasingly evident that things couldn't continue as they were. Different medications were tried to treat the UC but it was in vain as the symptoms remained infuriatingly unmanageable.

One morning, during the doctors rounds Mr Horton told me he was going to arrange a meeting with me and my parents to discuss a plan to move forward. I sensed that the situation was serious but I felt hopeful rather than scared. I just wanted to feel better.

The following afternoon we were waiting together in one of the dreary treatment rooms, the atmosphere was solemn and I could tell Mum and Dad were worried. Mr Horton arrived and sat down behind a large desk. Folding his hands together, he regarded me sternly with steely grey eyes. I felt as though I was sitting in from of a head teacher about to be chastised for misbehaving and unwelcome nerves fluttered in my tummy. He studies my hospital notes for a moment and when he looked up again his face was slightly softer.

'We are in a pickle aren't we Jennifer, his voice perversely loud in the quiet room. I didn't answer as it seemed this was a statement rather than a question.

Our options are rather limited I'm afraid. Medical treatments are not going to be sufficient to keep your Ulcerative Colitis in remission and I am sure you have had more than enough,' he sympathised.

Up until now I had managed to keep my emotions in check; his uncharacteristic kindness caused annoying tears to burn the back of my throat. I had grown accustomed to his usual abrupt and brisk manner so this change threw me. Unable to speak and irritated with myself for being such a baby, I firmly pushed down the urge to cry and just nodded as Mr Horton continued.

He explained that the best course of action was for me to undergo major surgery to remove my badly diseased colon (large bowel). The most positive aspect of going ahead with this surgery was that it would in affect cure the UC. I would no longer have a colon to be diseased and therefore, would no longer be unwell.

Unfortunately and as is usually the case with the UC, this wouldn't be by any means a straightforward solution. In fact for someone of my immaturity and age it would come at quite a high price. The surgery would leave me unable to pass poo through my bottom. After removing my colon the surgeons would have to bring the end of my small intestine out onto the surface of my abdomen to create an opening called an ileostomy.

All of my waste would pass through the ileostomy and be collected into a special, disposable bag placed directly on top. I would have to learn to take care of the ileostomy by emptying and changing the bag regularly. Although they were taking my colon they planned to leave my rectum in place. By doing so I would have the possible option of surgery to reverse the ileostomy when I reached full adult maturity.

'It is important that you understand Jennifer, future reversal surgery isn't guaranteed. There would be a lot to consider and sometimes it simply isn't possible. Until then you are going to have to learn to live with massive changes in your body. Given your age it isn't ideal,' said Mr Horton.

He went on to say that resolving my current situation was his main concern. The UC was making me dangerously unwell and it needed dealing with urgently.

I tried to take it all in. Mum and Dad were asking lots of questions but I had zoned out and their voices were distant. All I wanted was to be well again, how bad could this ileostomy thing be? It had to be better than the hours of painful diarrhoea and feeling so poorly. Anything would be preferable to being stuck in this shitty hospital.

So I would have to live with an ileostomy for at least three years. If after three years reversal surgery wasn't a feasible option for me then the remaining rectum would be removed and I would be left with a permanent ileostomy bag. It was hard to envisage where we would be in three days, let alone three years; it was all so overwhelming!

When Mr Horton explained all of this to us it was quite obvious that this surgery was urgent. It was also a necessity and not a choice; it was the only realistic option available to me.

Regardless of this Mr Horton insisted that we go away, talk about it and ask questions.

Over the next few days my parents and the nurses and doctors tried in vain to impress on me how life changing this massive surgery would be. It made no difference. I had completely latched onto to the fact the surgery would rid me of the UC and nothing else seemed significant. I would be well again, no more hospitals, no more painful, embarrassing diarrhoea, no more pancreatitis and no more medication.

I wanted to be a normal teenager and genuinely believed this was the perfect solution. All I needed to do was have surgery, get rid of the disease and live with a funny little bag on my tummy for a couple of years.

Surely it couldn't be that bad, I thought, conveniently disregarding the nagging doubts loitering in the back of my mind.

As soon as the decision had been made to go ahead and have the surgery everything seemed to happen very quickly. I was referred to the surgical team and met a surgeon called Mr James who would be carrying out the operation. I was also visited by a lady whose name was Carol.

Carol was a Specialist Stoma Care Nurse and her role was to help me manage the new ileostomy following surgery. She explained everything to me again and showed me the type of bag I would have to wear over the ileostomy. The bag would need to be emptied throughout the day and completely changed every three to four days.

'It will take a little time to get used to but you will soon learn how to manage,' said Carol.

She didn't need to sell it to me. I had convinced myself that this was the perfect solution; it certainly sounded preferable to more time in hospital.

I examined the bag Carol had handed me. It was a little bigger than I had imagined and was made of a soft plastic which was similar to my skin colour. On the back was an adhesive pad which would stick onto my skin covering the ileostomy and there was a clip on the bottom end which would hold the poo inside the bag until I emptied it. Carol showed me where it would sit on my tummy after the surgery and explained how the end would just tuck into my knickers.

'It will be very discreet. No one will have any idea it's there unless you want to tell them, explained Carol. You can even wear a swimming costume and it won't be visible,' she added. The beam on her face suggested that this was a special feature just for me!

It was strange to think I would have some kind of permanent "opening" in my tummy and I imagined it to be some sort of a tube leading into the bag. In all honesty my focus wasn't on the finer details. I just wanted to be better and if this was what it would take then that was fine by me!

While I wasn't too worried about managing afterwards I was quietly terrified at the prospect of having such a serious operation. I had my tonsils removed when I was younger but that was nothing compared to this. Pushing my fears aside I tried to focus on the fact I would be able to go home in a couple of weeks.

Despite having had everything explained to me in detail by Mr James and Carol I was actually extremely unprepared and totally ignorant to what was about to happen to my body. Maybe this was a blessing. Had I had foresight into the reality of life as a teenager with an ileostomy then I may not have been so eager to go ahead. It wasn't going to be the easy solution I was so naively anticipating!

Dad arranged to have some holiday from work as the day scheduled for surgery approached. I was glad because I could see how scared my mum was. She tried to hide it from me but the apprehension in her eyes was apparent. I believe she felt every single thing I was going through as if it were happening to her. Having to watch me endure it was probably so much worse.

'I wish I could do it for you sweetheart,' said Nan also feeling helpless.

They would have done anything to take it all away. I know they were worried about how I would cope afterwards with the ileostomy. I had decided it would be absolutely fine but then I was fed up of being ill and stuck in hospital. They sensed that it wasn't going to be as easy a transition as I pictured.

I hated to worry my family and I felt guilty knowing that the situation was causing them a lot of stress. It didn't matter how much of a cheerful façade they kept up, I wasn't fooled for a moment. My brother Bill was eight years old and it was all quite confusing and disruptive for him too. He begrudged the constant back and forth to the hospital; it was boring. He would fidget and moan through visiting. I would get irritated and resentful. He couldn't even visit for a couple of hours without complaining when I had been stuck in this bloody hospital for weeks!

He was just a little boy who wanted to be at home playing with his toys and watching his favourite television programmes. Nan looked after him as much as possible but there were occasions when he would have to come along with Mum to visit me. Ward Five wasn't a particularly pleasant environment; the air was often polluted with toilet odours. I had got used to it but Bill would wrinkle his nose up in disgust every time he came. He didn't like being surrounded by sick people, watching everyone stress and fawn over his big sister.

It was difficult for him to understand what was happening but he must have sensed the seriousness of it all. Sometimes he would give me an awkward hug before they left and I could detect his fear and uncertainty.

Mum was completely exhausted. She was still working full time running a busy school kitchen. As soon as she finished work she would come straight to the hospital to sit with me. It didn't matter how tired she was she always managed to keep a positive mask on while supporting me and entertaining Bill. It was physically and emotionally draining for everyone but it must have been hell for Mum.

The day before I was due to have surgery I was transferred onto Ward Two which was a specialist surgical ward. Despite generally loathing the hospital, I had grown accustomed to the ways and routine of Ward Five. It was really strange saying goodbye to the familiar faces of the nurses I had got to know so well during my stay. However, it was a step closer to getting home so mixed in with my unease at leaving them was excitement and nervous anticipation.

A porter called Bob collected me and my belonging. He wasn't one for conversation which I was glad of as I didn't much feel like talking. He whistled noisily as he expertly steered me through the long hospital corridors to my new home. As we entered Ward Two there was a nurse sitting at the desk, her head buried in a mountain of files and paperwork.

'New inmate for you,' Bob bellowed before continuing on with his tuneless whistling.

She flinched in obvious annoyance at being interrupted.

'Yes put her on B3 for now please,' instructed the nurse glancing up briefly.

'Righty Ho,' said Bob knocking over a bin as he clumsily manoeuvred my bed to its allocated spot.

He winked at me and sniggered as the nurse failed to conceal her irritation at his slapdash ways. I could have sworn he made a point of whistling extra loudly as he passed her on his way out; I liked Bob!

There was only two other patients near to me and they were both fast asleep, attached to machines which were bleeping and humming intermittently. I was alone and was immediately struck by how different the atmosphere was here. Instead of bays the ward was larger and more open with the nurse's station positioned right in the middle. Ward Two was located in the slightly more modern area of the hospital. Everything was bright white and clean which was a stark contrast to Ward Five with its rattily windows and shabby peeling walls.

I began unpacking and rearranging my things to give me something to do. That didn't take long so I lay back on the bed and tried to read my book. It was impossible to concentrate and after reading the same paragraph multiple times I gave up.

Eventually the sullen nurse came and went through some paperwork to admit me to the ward. After that I didn't see anyone until Mum and Dad arrived at tea time and I was so relieved to see their familiar faces I immediately burst into tears.

'It's strange here, I don't like it,' I sobbed as Mum tried to reassure me that I would soon be used to it.

The tears relieved the pressure cooker of emotions which had been building up all day and I felt better. Despite wanting to chat with my parents after feeling so bewildered all day, their visit unfortunately coincided with my pre-op assessment. The anaesthetist who would be looking after me throughout the surgery came to assess me first.

Every surgery which requires a general anaesthetic carries certain risks and it is standard procedure to ensure that the patient is aware. As the anaesthetist ran through a checklist of the potential risk factors I began to feel even more anxious.

There were two things which really terrified me. The first was that I might die, which is a reasonable concern when faced with major surgery. So when the anaesthetist listed death as a (highly unlikely) risk, fear struck me like a speeding train. Not wanting to be perceived as immature, I tried to mask how scared I was. Mum's hand was clamped tightly to mine and communicated not only that she knew exactly how I was feeling, but that she was frightened too.

My second fear wasn't actually listed by the anaesthetist but this didn't prevent me from fretting about it. I had recently read a magazine article about a woman who claimed to have regained consciousness during surgery. She disclosed that she had woken up and been aware of everything but was completely paralysed and unable to alert the surgeon to her plight. What if this happened to me!?

Rationally I knew that this was extremely unlikely and I thought I would seem silly if I asked for reassurance. The hospital staff treated me as an adult despite my young age and this resulted in me often being unable to communicate just how overwhelmed I was. It always seemed wrong to make a fuss.

So as I had on so many occasions, I simply pretended I was fine. This didn't stop the terrifying scenario of waking up mid surgery playing over and over in my mind! The torment was so great I found myself turning to an old OCD ritual in an attempt to dampen my anxiety. The particular ritual I used was to repeat The Lord's Prayer in my head seven times. If I made a mistake or was interrupted I would have to start again.

Those were the strange conditions set out by my frightened mind and each time I felt scared the process was repeated. While the use of rituals to combat anxiety usually only exacerbates the issues in the long term, these were intense and difficult circumstances. If relentlessly reciting a prayer in my head was going to help me through then I certainly wasn't going to resist!

Before my parents went home Mr James and his team arrived to go over the surgery one final time and to get the consent form signed. As I was a minor it was down to Mum to sign with my agreement and she did so with a shaky hand. It was beginning to sink in for us all that this was really happening.

Mr James drew a large X in a black marker pen on my belly explaining that this was where the ileostomy would be positioned. It seemed such a peculiar thing to do and I wanted to laugh. It was all so surreal like a weird dream where a man in a white coat was using my abdomen as an art canvas.

'X marks the spot,' Mum said bringing me back to reality.

Dad ruffled my hair affectionately as they got ready to leave me for the night. I could tell that neither of them really wanted to go, talking to the anaesthetist and surgeon had unsettled us all.

'Na-night Jen, big day tomorrow,' chirped Mum a little too brightly.

Her nonchalance was unconvincing. I knew it was just a front and that she was trying to be brave for me; the smile painted on her face failed to conceal the worry in her eyes.

It was getting late and the night shift had arrived. I tried to rest but couldn't get comfortable. Every time I shifted my position the bed creaked and complained loudly. The ward carried a serious atmosphere and the night time silence amplified it. I didn't want to draw attention to myself or disturb anyone so I lay frozen and uncomfortable, almost afraid to breathe. The other two patients near me were both sleeping soundly and I envied their peace. Aside from the occasional noise from a blood pressure machine or the gentle footsteps of a nurse, the silence was deafening.

My thoughts drifted back to tomorrow's surgery and resulted in a violent surge of panic; the redundant adrenaline alerting my body to a non-existent threat. Squeezing my eyes tightly shut I began the trusted repetition of The Lord's Prayer to seek relief. My panic began to evaporate as the ritual had the desired effect and somewhere between "Give us this day our daily bread" and "Amen" I drifted into a grateful slumber.

A Life Changing Day

Rudely awakened by the bright lights on the ward, I lay for a moment and on becoming more conscious remembered what the day had in store. I was first on the operating list so although it was quite early there wasn't time to lie in bed thinking and worrying. The day staff had already arrived and formed a group at the nurse's station.

A young nurse broke away from the others and came over to me. I was immediately struck by how pretty she was with shiny dark hair hanging from the nape of her neck in a flawlessly poker straight ponytail. Her eye lashes were thick and luxurious and framed her large almond eyes perfectly.

I felt so disgustingly drab and smelly after sweating profusely during the night and found myself wishing I looked as fresh and pretty as the nurse in front of me.

'Mornin, I'm Laura and I'll be looking after you today. How you doing?' the dimple in her cheek danced prettily as she spoke. Without waiting for me to answer she continued.

'Nervous huh?'

I nodded dumbly, too overwhelmed to speak and embarrassed as fresh tears stung my eyes.

'Hey now, what's all this? Just think, by the end of today it'll all be over,' she said putting her arm around me.

'I know. I'm ok,' I murmured wiping the tears away with the back of my hand and forcing a brave smile.

'That's more like it,'

Satisfied that she had reassured me, Laura handed me a fresh hospital gown and a pair of tight white surgical stockings.

'Now then, your bath is ready. Go and have a quick dip, use this bar of soap. You can't have any bubbles in the water and you mustn't use any talc or lotion either, it's important you have no residue on your skin when you go for surgery. I will help you with the stockings afterwards, alright?'

She bustled around, chivvying me along. Her affable, no nonsense manner reminded me of Mary Poppins; I almost expected to hear the words "Spit Spot".

Wondering how she could behave as though it was such an ordinary day when I was filled with such trepidation I obediently headed to the bathroom. Floating in the unperfumed bath water I tried to relax. It was so blissful; I wished that I could just stay immersed in the soothing heat rather than face the day.

After ten minutes, mindful that I probably shouldn't take too long I reluctantly climbed out, dried and pulled on the gown. Wearing a gown instead of one of my own comfortable nighties emphasized the reality of what I was about to face.

The bathroom was steamy and hot so despite having had a good wash I didn't feel particularly fresh. Conscious of my lack of underwear I firmly gripped the opening at the back of the gown as I wandered back to my bed. Exposing my bare bum to the other patients was an avoidable disgrace.

My hair was damp with sweat so I tied it messily up on top of my head in an attempt to cool down. Then Nurse Laura reappeared to help me on with the horrendously tight stockings. She also had to shave away the top part of my pubic hair. It was funny to think that six months ago I would have been absolutely mortified by this intimate procedure. Either I had become completely immune to the embarrassment or I was far too nervous to care.

The glaring black cross marking the ileostomy site was hard to ignore. It contaminated the soft pink of my skin and I unwittingly found myself wondering what it would look like after the surgery. It was so hard to imagine. I knew I would have an opening which would lead into a bag of some sort but I had absolutely no idea what it would look like or how it would feel.

Laura finished prepping me for theatre and disappeared for a time. Left to my own devices I got back into bed. Nearby patients were dozing and the peaceful atmosphere didn't match the cloud of anxiety and unease surrounding me.

Just as the fear and anticipation of the day ahead was becoming unbearable Mum and Dad arrived. It was such a huge relief; their familiarity going some way to silencing my nerves.

There was an air of forced cheeriness which we didn't acknowledge. Dad was making daft jokes and Mums' eyes were bright and shiny as though tears were close. We chatted away about anything and nothing for the next hour. As the time for my surgery drew closer, the atmosphere between the three of us felt almost manic.

It was half an hour before I was due to go when Nurse Laura gave me a couple of tablets, she called them a pre-med. Before long I had drifted into a welcome state of relaxation. Turning to Mum I slurred…

'My insides feel like cotton wool.'

She laughed obviously grateful that I was more peaceful. I comfortably dozed on and off until movement and voices around the bed brought me around. Realising the porter had arrived to wheel me to the operating theatre; I lurched from my tranquil state. Suddenly time seemed to be moving quickly.

I manoeuvred awkwardly onto the uncomfortable trolley while trying in vain to secure the gaping hospital gown! Hospital notes were plonked down by my feet and all of my drips were taken from the stands and placed next to me. Nurse Laura was coming with us and before we left the ward she checked my ID bracelet and asked me my date of birth along with some other random questions about metal work in my body and loose teeth! Even though I wasn't feeling particularly cold I began to shiver. The porter noticed and kindly placed another blanket over my legs.

It was time to go. Mum and Dad walked with us along the breezy corridors until we reached the lift and Laura said this was as far as they could come. I could see they were both upset and didn't want to leave me. I forced a smile as I kissed them goodbye thinking,

I hope I see you again…..I hope I don't die.

'We will be waiting for you on the ward Jen, it will soon be all over,' said Mum as if reading my mind.

They tried to hide it but I knew they were scared too; scared and helpless. Seeing my parents fear was worse than my own, it was unbearable. The calm supplied by the pre-med was evaporating as I was wheeled into the lift. Giving a casual wave as the doors closed I tried to appear unaffected. As soon as Mum and Dad disappeared out of sight the dam broke and tears flowed. This was really happening.

Travelling in a lift is a really weird experience on a trolley. The sensation of moving upwards while lying flat is unusual. The porter and the nurse were chatting but I was in my own world not particularly listening.

As the porter pushed me through the double doors into the theatre reception it was eerily quiet unlike the chaos of the wards. Two people greeted to us. Their uniforms were different to the standard attire worn by the ward staff; instead they sported murky green tunics and trousers and had surgical masks looped around their necks. On their feet were (almost unnaturally clean) white clogs; these were a stark contrast to the conventional black lace up shoes donned by the majority of the nurses.

Bizarrely the clogs made me think of the country dancers I had grown up watching at our towns' carnival. Every year we would meet as a family at Great Nan's house for a buffet tea after watching the procession of flamboyantly decorated floats.

Then we got to go to the fair for a few hours. It was the best time, full of sticky candyfloss and amber toffee apples able to break a tooth in one bite. The noise of the rides and people screaming in a combination of terror and delight created a fun, colourful vibe. Even after our buffet tea, the delicious smells coming from the burger vans; fried onions, smoky hot dogs and chips swimming in vinegar would make me drool longingly.

This was soon blotted out by the inevitable sight of someone puking. There was always more than one fool who believed they could indulge in a greasy burger before spinning wildly on The Waltzers!

The happy memories created warmth inside me. I closed my eyes for a moment wishing I was anywhere but here when Nurse Laura saying goodbye jolted me back to reality. Watching her retreating back through the double doors I felt alone. The feeling didn't have time to take root as one of the clogged ladies began asking me some questions.

It was strangely intimidating, this stranger in a surgical mask, towering above me and asking the same set of questions I had already answered. It added to the intensity and the fear. When I recall these moments it surprises me just how sharp the memories are. It is as though I am being attacked by the past; each blow as acute and painful as it was then.

I answered the nurses' questions momentarily uncertain of my answers. I didn't think I had any loose teeth or caps but what if I did and didn't know? What would happen to me?

'We have to make sure we have the right person,' the nurse said, mistaking my doubt for impatience.

Half of me wished she would stop talking and just get on with it, the other half happy to delay the inevitable. When they finally took me into the anaesthetic room and began attaching me to the monitoring equipment panic really began to take hold. It took every bit of strength I had not to jump off the trolley and run; I was actually trembling with fear.

The anaesthetist was lovely and tried to distract me with questions about school and pop music. Panic got the better of me.

'I'm scared I'm going to wake up in the middle of the operation!' I blurted out.

'That isn't going to happen Jennifer I promise, I will be monitoring you the whole time,' the anaesthetist said squeezing my hand reassuringly.

I took a deep breath as the anaesthetist began injecting some creamy liquid into the needle in my hand. A mask was placed over my face and I started to freak out a little.

'It's ok. Count backwards from ten, you will start to feel sleepy now.'

My fear began to fade and the top of my head felt tingly. I counted….ten…nine unable to get any further than eight as the darkness swallowed me.

It seemed as though I fell asleep and awoke again as quickly as a light switch being turned off and on. I felt disorientated; there were voices and bleeping noises. My mouth was dry causing my lips to stick together and there was a mask over my face. This slightly claustrophobic sensation caused me to automatically reach up and move it away. Almost immediately someone had placed it gently but firmly back in position.

'It's just oxygen Jennifer, you need to leave it there,' a voice said.

The haziness was lifting and things were beginning to get a little clearer now. I focused on the face looking down at me and recognised it was Nurse Laura.

'Welcome back!' she said smiling. The realisation that the ordeal was over enveloped me like a warm hug! It was such a relief I almost couldn't believe it. My dad appeared then and took hold of my hand. I was so happy to see him.

'I love you,' I murmured drowsily.

I had been in the operating theatre for almost eight hours and it had been a long and stressful wait for my parents. A combination of relief and distress had overwhelmed my mum when she saw me back on the ward attached to numerous drips, drains and machines. My temperature had dropped so I was also wrapped in some kind of silver foil blanket. I must have looked quite a sight. To avoid me witnessing her anguish, Mum had gone for a coffee with Carol the Stoma Care Nurse but I was far too out of it to notice.

'Are you in any pain,' asked Nurse Laura.

I shook my head no as sleepiness took over. My tummy was sore but the strong painkillers given during the operation were doing their job. I drifted in and out of consciousness not really aware of anything happening around me. The blood pressure cuff would occasionally go tight on my arm and the oxygen mask still felt a little stifling but aside from that I was reasonably comfortable.

Unable to keep my eyes open I slept and each time I awoke things had changed. The first time I stirred, Mum and Dad were sitting by my bed. I mumbled hello to Mum as she lovingly stroked my cheek. Then I dozed again. The next time I awoke they had gone home. It was dark so I knew it was night time but had no idea of the actual time. I must have fallen asleep again because the next thing I knew two nurses were trying to rouse me in order to change my bed sheets.

'We just need to clean you up a bit sweetie, one nurse coaxed. Can you roll over onto your side for me please?'

All I wanted to do was sleep but knowing they wouldn't take no for an answer, begrudgingly decided to cooperate. Up until this point aside from occasionally moving my arms to pull at the annoying oxygen mask; I had pretty much remained in the same position. So other than a little discomfort, I hadn't experienced any real pain. I was totally unprepared for just how excruciating rolling over would be.

Every movement was agony; as though a hundred knives were piercing my tummy. Even shifting my legs caused a painful pulling sensation and by the time the sheet underneath me was changed I was crying, desperately wishing they would stop and leave me alone.

'Use your morphine if it's hurting,' the nurse reminded me.

Pressing the button down on the morphine pump I waited for it to ease my suffering. It didn't seem to help at all. Aware of my distress, the nurses worked as quickly and gently as they could. They managed to wash me and completely change my sheets without having to get me out of bed once. It was quite impressive but unfortunately I was in too much pain to appreciate their skills!

While they were washing me I became aware of something adhesive being pulled off of my lower tummy. There was a warm sensation as the area was wiped clean. A strong smell of poo raided my nostrils and it dawned on me that they were changing the ileostomy bag. Bile rose in my throat as I resisted the urge to vomit. Feeling terrified of what I might see should I look down I was becoming increasingly agitated.

'Can you stop now....it's making me feel sick,' I pleaded.

After what seemed like an eternity they finally finished with me and I was gratefully left to sleep. However the hazy bliss of the anaesthetic had begun to dissipate. The pain caused by rolling over was lingering and I was uncomfortable and upset.

Not wanting to move in case the pain got any worse I lay completely still. The more I tried to focus on anything other than my sore tummy, the more it throbbed! It was impossible. After an hour of not moving and pressing my morphine pump button continuously I rang my call bell and sobbed to the nurse.

'I will see if you are written up for anything else ok?' she said with an understanding smile.

I could have kissed her when she returned a few minutes later with some more pain relief. It wasn't long before I felt the effects and floated back into a peaceful slumber. This pattern continued for the next twenty four hours. I would sleep for a few hours, wake up in pain, be given pain relief, fall asleep and repeat.

When Mum and Nan visited me I only managed to stay awake long enough to say hello. I don't remember but apparently Nan began telling me a story about her allotment and I dozed off half way through it! She never let me forget that one, the time her gardening tales bored me to sleep! Needless to say, now that my pain was better controlled I was a lot happier.

Maybe I will just sleep until I'm healed I thought optimistically.

However much I wanted that scenario to play out I was soon to discover my recovery wasn't going to be that easy. After a day of being allowed to relax in a peaceful drug induced fog, the rude awakening came......I was made to get up!

As I had found the task of rolling onto my side painful it wasn't surprising that actually getting out of bed was much worse! Somehow, the nurses helped me to move to the side of the bed into a sitting position. This in itself was a juggling act due to the various tubes and drips located about my person.

I had a catheter to empty my urine, a surgical drain in my tummy as well as a drip in my arm and my feeding tube. I was suddenly very aware of all these "attachments" because along with three surgical wounds (one of which was the entire length of my abdomen) they were causing painful pulling sensations. Every single movement felt as though my tender skin was being split open. With one nurse holding the catheter and drain bags and the other supporting me, I managed to stand.

'Take your time now; it's been a few days since you were on your feet. It's quite common to feel a bit dizzy," warned the nurse firmly gripping my arm.

Feeling weak and pathetic, I tentatively took the four small steps to the chair by my bed. The position of the catheter and drain heightened the discomfort of the cold plastic armchair. Tired, sore and emotional, all I wanted was to get back into the bed. The wrinkled sheets and sweaty plastic pillows suddenly so inviting.

One of the nurses presented me with a bowl of soapy water and helped me to have a wash and put on a clean nightie. It was ridiculously exhausting even to wash my face but the comfort of putting on one of my own soft nighties made up for it.

I still wouldn't look down at my tummy; too weak and emotionally fragile to even have a glance. Feeling fresher after my wash I shifted slightly hoping to find a more comfortable position on the slippery chair. This proved to be a waste of time and moving was still painful so I stayed still and pressed my morphine pump instead.

My eyes were heavy and my head felt like a concrete block balanced on my shoulders. I knew I would have to just grin and bear it but my wallowing mood was making it extremely difficult to stay positive. One of the nurses had explained, sympathetically but firmly that I needed to sit up for at least an hour.

*It's alright for her; it's going to be sodding torture sitting like this for an hour....*I thought irritably.

Feeling so dreadfully tired was excruciating. There was nowhere to rest my head comfortably in the chair so I daringly tried to reach over and grab a pillow from the bed. This arrogant attempt at independence provoked such agony I gave up immediately. Tears of frustration and pain soaked my cheeks. I surrendered and leaned back in the chair, glaring senselessly at the pillows as if they had deliberately chosen to be out of reach.

The Physio-Terrorist

I had been sitting uncomfortably for a while when a young man in a white uniform approached me.

'Hi there, my name is Steven. I'm one of the physiotherapy team, how are you feeling today?

'Sore,' I grunted hoping that my short response might get rid of him.

He was actually really good looking with dark hair and a nice smile. Not that his level of attractiveness mattered, I couldn't be bothered with anyone or anything.

'Ahh that's to be expected. Your body has just been through a massive trauma,' his face conveying sympathy as he spoke.

Although uninvited Steven sat on the edge of the bed and explained that after such major surgery I was at risk of developing certain complications.

'We worry about things like a chest infection and blood clots. These things are more of a risk if you don't get moving after your surgery. Which is why those evil nurses will be making you get up every day,' he said with a chuckle.

He seemed like such a nice man and was obviously trying to thaw out the icy atmosphere my mood was creating. For some reason, the nicer he was to me the more petulant and ratty I became! Not letting my obvious disgust at his presence deter him, Steven said that to recover quickly I would need to do some special exercises every day.

Well this was news to me! The idea of exercising made my heart sink; there was absolutely no way I could manage it! My depressed mood turned to panic as visions of jumping jacks and press ups ran through my exhausted mind. As ignoring Steven wasn't working, I decided to change tack and whimpered pathetically......

'What, you want me to do exercises *today*?'

He laughed at my obvious incredulity.

'Don't worry Jennifer; these exercises are so simple you can do them sitting in your chair. You can even have a nice cup of tea afterwards,' he wheedled.

There was determination etched all over his handsome face. In a last ditch attempt to appeal to his compassionate side I began to cry.

'I really don't think I can yet – it hurts even to move.'

My pitiful tears made little impression on the man in front of me.

'I'll tell you what, I will ask the nurses if you can have some more pain relief and then we will just work together for ten minutes ok? I know it's hard but it is important that you try.'

The sympathy in his voice was accompanied by a no nonsense tone. Tears and tantrums were not going to change my plight; Steven and his sodding exercises were going nowhere. Having made my unwillingness crystal clear, Steven's patience had to be commended. I tried hard to be amicable but it was a struggle. As soon as we began the exercises my loathing towards this stranger grew to a level which shocked me.

The first task seemed relatively easy. All I had to do was take a deep breath in and blow into a plastic tube contraption. There was a small ball in the bottom and the aim was to puff hard enough to push it to the top of the tube. It is astonishing to believe that something so simple could cause so much pain. My abdominal muscles had taken quite a battering during the surgery. Taking a deep breath in was sore and exhaling quickly hurt like hell!

Hoping to satisfy (and get rid of) this nagging man I gave it my all. I genuinely tried but it just seemed to go on forever. The first exercise alone exceeded the promised ten minute limit with Steven making me repeat it relentlessly. Not only was he annoying, (and confusingly attractive) he was a liar. I bloody hated him!

When the first round of torturous exercises was complete there was little time to recover. Steven had another activity lined up for me.

'All you have to do is sit up straight, hold this pillow against your tummy and cough as hard as you can,' he said demonstrating with an impressive deep cough.

Given how tough blowing into a tube had been I don't know why I was gullible enough to think that coughing would be easy. Oh the pain, it was unbelievable. I must have looked a truly pathetic and disgusting sight and I felt embarrassed. Steven was clean and fresh. He was healthy, full of energy and sickening enthusiasm. My hair hadn't been washed for weeks and clung to my head like oily rats tails. The surgical stockings were grubby and I was surrounded by bags of my own bodily fluids.

Hugging the pillow as though my life depended on it I forced myself to cough. Angry tears scorched my face. I was sporting a more deathly white than my usual shade of pale which made the crimson streaks especially prominent. I knew I looked horrendous and this alongside my inability to control my emotions was extremely humiliating.

A chest infection or a blood clot would have been disastrous and potentially life threatening but at that moment nothing would have convinced me that these activities were valuable. I have never been a confrontational person but I was fast reaching my limit. Glaring at Steven through blurry eyes I snapped,

'I'm not doing any more now! Go away!'

The anger in my voice was so unnatural it shocked me. Steven didn't even flinch; he just smiled easily and helped me get back into bed.

'You did really well dear, it'll get easier. Try not to give up,' he urged.

I sank appreciatively into the pillows which were soft as marshmallows. Even though Steven was still talking to me I turned my head away and shut my eyes. It was a deliberately petulant gesture which I hoped would convey my loathing for him and his stupid exercises. The next time I looked, he was gone.

The first few days following my surgery were grim to say the least. Every day the nurses and physio would push me to do a little more when all I wanted was to be left alone to rest. If it wasn't physical pain preventing me from cooperating it was sheer exhaustion. At times I wondered if I would ever feel well again, even cleaning my teeth or brushing my hair left me as weak as a new-born kitten!

It was on day three post-surgery when a surprise delivery arrived. Despite pleading with the nurses to stay in bed I found myself perched precariously on the "torture chair" again. My mood was predictably low and I was emotional and cranky. The usual ward routine was in process with staff milling about while I glared angrily at no one in particular, counting down the minutes until I could return to bed.

Mid-morning a florist came onto the ward which wasn't particularly unusual. Not paying any attention I continued to fidget and sulk. It was only when the florist placed the basket of flowers down on my table I realised that this delivery was for me!

I gazed in surprise at the stunning display in front of me. The wicker basket was bursting with plump red roses. Interspersed among the velvet petals were sprays of tiny white flowers. They peppered the crimson blooms like gentle snowflakes. The handle of the basket was wrapped in satin ribbon which shimmered in the light. It all looked so vibrant and fresh it seemed out of place on the dismal hospital ward. Tucked in among the delicately scented flowers was a card which I pulled out tentatively so not to disturb the perfect display.

"Hello my Jen,
I wanted you to have something just as beautiful as you. Take your time; slow and steady wins the race.
Love you always, Nan."

Predictably the tears flowed but even though I was crying something inside me lifted. The familiar sight of Nan's elegant cursive handwriting made me feel less lonely and just that little bit stronger. My boosted spirits even took the nurses by surprise, especially when I agreed to sit up a while longer with no complaints. Thanks to Nan's perfectly timed flowers I managed an impressive twenty more minutes in the torture chair that morning!

Initially the nursing staff appreciated my reluctance to see the results of my surgery. If the ileostomy bag needed changing it was done for me while I made a conscious effort not to look. I was aware that unless I planned on remaining in hospital forever it was something I would ultimately have to face. So after being afforded a few days of happy avoidance, the time to have a look at my poor mangled tummy arrived. There was no denying that I was extremely nervous at the prospect, but mixed in with the apprehension was curiosity. Despite myself, I actually wanted to have a little look.

Carol the Specialist Stoma Care Nurse had taken me into one of the bathrooms. I was sitting on the toilet seat lid and she rolled up my nightie and using a washing peg fastened it out of the way.

'That's not for my nose then?' I laughed, attempting to appear upbeat and blasé.

Carol just smiled and carried on laying things out. There was some white gauze, sterile water and a tube of cream. The clean ileostomy bag was also there. It was round at the top and tapered down into a neck, a bit like the shape of a lightbulb only it was flat.

'Do you think you ready to have a look then dear? Carol asked laying a towel over my knees. That's all you need to do today. I will see to everything else.'

Having no idea what to expect I tentatively glanced down. My tummy still had a yellow tinge from the iodine solution used to clean the area before the surgery. This unexpected glow gave me a slight jolt and my pulse surged. There were a vertical row of neat stitches the length of my abdomen and the tubes for the drain and catheter were also sewn in place. It was quite a mess but gaining confidence my eyes surveyed the damage. Like a rubbernecker; curiosity compelled me to look even though I was certain it was a bad idea!

I hadn't a clue what the ileostomy would look like and up until this moment had not allowed myself to imagine. Stuck to the lower right of my tummy was a bag. Unlike the fresh bag Carol had laid out this one was completely transparent so the ileostomy was impossible to miss. Nothing could have prepared me for the sight of it.

Part of my small intestine was now on the outside of my body via a surgical opening to the right of my navel. It was just sitting there; a strange alien blob. Bizarrely my first thought was that it looked as though someone had chopped a tinned tomato in half and stuck it onto my tummy! A mixture of both repulsion and fascination made it impossible for me to avert my eyes. Realising that Carol was speaking to me I looked up.

'Are you ok Jenny, you have gone very pale? Her voice was full of concern. Remember, everything is still quite swollen at the moment. That's all perfectly normal and will settle down,'

I didn't answer; the shock of my battered abdomen had rendered me temporarily mute. Looking at the ileostomy again I noticed the transparent bag contained some liquid which was a mixture of brown and spinach green. Realising it was poo I suddenly felt sick.

How could she say this was perfectly normal? Nothing about this was normal. It was disgusting!

A little lower down just above my pubis there was another dressing which Carol removed. It had been covering something called a mucus fistula. As there was a possibility that I could have reversal surgery in the future my rectum had been left in place. A mucus fistula is formed when the two ends of the bowel are bought out onto the surface of the abdomen. One is formed to pass the faeces (the ileostomy) and the other to release mucous produced by the disconnected end of the bowel (the fistula).

The fistula had a special cover to collect any discharge. Along with the ileostomy bag this would also need regularly changing. I was starting to wonder how on earth I was going to manage all of this without help. It was such a hot mess.

Sensing Carol's eyes on me I could see her trying to read my face. She was clearly a little troubled by the fact I hadn't spoken since the unveiling of my "car crash" tummy.

'Perhaps that's enough for today. Let me just change the bag and you can go back to bed for a rest. It's all a bit overwhelming.' she said.

I nodded in agreement and Carol patted my hand. Slowly, she began to remove the ileostomy bag by gently peeling the gummy adhesive away from my skin. In one swift movement she disposed of the old bag and placed a large square of gauze just underneath this "thing" on my tummy.

It was at that moment the smell became noticeable and boy was it strong! The potency hit me like festering sewage on a hot day! Fighting the urge to hold my nose I concentrated on breathing through my mouth instead.

Suddenly the ileostomy spluttered like a tiny volcano and expelled some more of the muddy liquid poo. It seeped onto the white gauze like a polluted river bursting its' banks. There was a warm sensation as some dribbled onto my skin. That was all it took; I began to heave violently.

Handing me a cardboard bowl Carol gently rubbed my back for a moment. The sight and smell of the ileostomy was utterly repellent to me and the uncontrollable retching agony. It was such a relief when the clean bag was in place and I could finally breathe without dry heaving.

It wasn't until Carol was helping me back into bed that the enormity of the situation hit me. I began to cry. Not just a little weep either, loud wretched sobs emerged from deep inside. It was so embarrassing but I couldn't stop. Carol just sat quietly beside me until the worst was over and I was just letting out the odd tearful hiccup.

'Better?' she asked handing me a warm flannel to wash my face.

"Yes thanks,' I gulped holding the soothing cloth over my eyes.

The feeling of peace that follows a good cry was coming over me and I was calmer.

'You know it's perfectly normal to react like that Jenny, in fact I think it was needed, assured Carol gently. Things will get easier from now, the worst is over I promise.'

Totally drained I lay back on the bed. Sensing Carol wanted more of a response I managed a watery smile.

'You will soon be able to look after the ileostomy by yourself. It just takes a little practice but you'll be a pro in no time" she added.

Afterwards, when I was alone I stared into space trying to process everything. Carol seemed certain that I was going to be able to manage the ileostomy myself eventually. While I hoped she was right it seemed incomprehensible. I never wanted to see it again, let alone clean it or touch it! The very idea made me shudder.

I closed my eyes in a veiled attempt to block out what I had seen. The image of my butchered tummy was still dancing around my minds' eye as I fell asleep.

As it turned out there was more to my extreme reaction on seeing the ileostomy than straightforward shock. The tube I had in place to supply me with nutrition had become infected. This was realised when the awful retching returned and rapidly evolved into vomiting. Every gag pulling so painfully on my stiches it was difficult to establish what was making my eyes stream more!

Shivering uncontrollably, I pulled a sheet up to my chin to warm up. It seemed the relentless puking wasn't torture enough. The sadistic nurses had confiscated my blankets and aimed a fan at me. The infected tube was removed and I began a course of antibiotics.

While this experience was unpleasant it was more of an inconvenience than a catastrophe. These sorts of infections are relatively common after such extensive surgery. My body had been through the mill, making me weaker and more susceptible. The antibiotics worked efficiently and after a couple of grim days and I began to feel much better. I was overjoyed when the doctors decided it was time to have my catheter and drain removed. As long as I managed to eat and drink a little more the final drip could also come down. It was all a step closer to getting home!

There was still one huge hurdle to overcome before I could escape and become an outpatient. No matter how much I had tried to ignore the obvious I needed to be able to care for the ileostomy independently.

Physically I had really turned a corner and this in itself had drastically improved my mood. I was feeling stronger, more positive and simply desperate to go home. Now that I was beginning to heal the hospital environment was becoming increasingly stifling. It had been over two months since my admission and I wanted out! For this to happen I knew I would have to face the ileostomy again.

So a week after I had seen my new body (and vowed never to look at again) I found myself back in the little bathroom with Carol. Ready for round two!

This time I was not only going to look at the ileostomy but attempt to change the bag myself! I was nervous but it felt different this time. Now the initial shock had died down, I knew what to expect. All the same I was secretly glad of Carol's presence, reassured that she would take over if I couldn't manage.

Carol was absolutely amazing! Not only was she a much needed calming influence, she was also incredibly organised. Everything I possibly needed to complete the task was laid out in front of me and she had talked me through each item and even written it all down!

Taking a deep breath, I began to peel back the sticky adhesive of the soiled ileostomy bag. Once it was removed I placed in into the rubbish bag and then unsure what to do for a moment I glanced at Carol who nodded and smiled before handing me a large square of gauze.

Placing this underneath the ileostomy to catch any discharge I squeezed some saline onto another square and with shaking hands began cleaning the area. The room was so quiet as I concentrated you could have heard the proverbial pin drop. I didn't realise I was holding my breath until Carol's voice broke the silence reminding me to exhale.

'Don't be frightened to touch it Jenny. I know it feels strange but your skin needs a good clean. You won't do any damage I promise. Your ileostomy is tougher than it looks,' she added.

Her words were encouraging but I was only half listening, totally transfixed by the pulsating wound on my tummy. It was astonishing that after my previous reaction I was even looking at it, let alone touching it! I was on some kind of auto pilot with determination as the driving force!

Despite gaining confidence I was very aware that a job which took Carol five minutes was taking me much longer. Ten minutes in and I was quickly discovering just how fiddly and messy this task was. The exposed ileostomy had suddenly decided to become very active. It was so frustrating because no sooner had I cleaned the surrounding area it would splutter and leak causing me to start again.

I was still gagging every time poo was expelled which added to the difficulty. Carol insisted that this would ease with time. Eventually the leaking subsided and I was able to get the area completely clean.

Next I needed to apply some thick sticky paste onto the skin around the edge of the ileostomy. This would act as a barrier to protect my skin and also help the fresh bag to stick firmly in place. Again, this was a finicky job as the paste seemed to stick everywhere except the area for which it was intended. Once it was "sort of" applied I positioned the clean bag over the top of the ileostomy. Holding it in place for a moment (the warmth of my hands would help the adhesive bond to my skin) I looked up at Carol and grinned in delight.

'I did it!' I exclaimed.

Carol laughed at my disbelief.

'You were brilliant, not that I doubted you for a moment! For the first go at changing the bag you did really well,' Carol said beaming back at me.

So that was that! I wasn't anywhere near as proficient at changing the bag as Carol. Start to finish the process had taken me nearly forty five minutes. It didn't matter. I had done it! Having recovered from the infection meant I had a slightly stronger stomach. Yes I was still heaving a little at the smell. The sight of my tummy was overwhelming but it was all beginning to feel slightly more bearable.

This was a big deal considering that just a few days earlier I had been adamant that I would never be able to cope. Maybe it was the thought of getting home that had given me the push and determination to try again. Not that the why really mattered, I knew I had taken a huge step forward and was absolutely euphoric!

When Mum and Nan visited that evening I was bursting to tell them of my achievement. I was verging on manic; probably because I could finally see a light at the end of the tunnel. Seeing how overexcited I was Mum suggested we sit in the day room for a change of scenery.

Glad to escape the oppressive atmosphere of the ward, I gripped Mum's arm tightly as we made our way along the corridor. Moving around was so much easier without all the tubes and drains; I felt less restricted. There was still a little pulling and soreness from my healing scar which made me walk quite tentatively but Mum and Nan walked slowly with me.

We finally got there and settled in some chairs with the TV on in the background. There was a comedy sketch show on and one of the characters was unwell and making some quite dramatic and exaggerated retching noises. I laughed and joked to Mum

'That was me a couple of days ago!'

Nan pulled a disapproving face; she could be a little stuffy at times.

'What disgusting behaviour,' she tutted.

Her disdain had a peculiar effect on Mum and I and we began to laugh. Soon we were in absolute hysterics and couldn't stop.

'I don't know what you are finding so funny,' said Nan which obviously made us worse.

Eventually Nan was laughing with us although she didn't really know why! It was like an explosion, weeks of stress; tension and pain were being released. They didn't stay for much longer as the merriments of the evening had left me resembling a wet rag. Laughing had felt so good but in my state, hysterical belly laughter was hard work! It was probably good physiotherapy though! I went to bed that night feeling sore and tired but happier than I had been for ages.

Annoyingly my elevated mood didn't accompany me into the following day and I awoke feeling quite weak and tearful. There was no reason for it as far as I knew; this hurricane of emotions was confusing.

There was an aspect of the day I was looking forward to however! Mum was coming in after breakfast so that Carol and I could show her the ileostomy and the process of changing the bag. I was mostly excited because this meant I wouldn't have to wait until visiting time to see her. They were so strict about adhering to visiting hours that I usually had to wait until four in the afternoon to see a familiar face. It made the days very long and dull.

Mum arrived and with Carol's guidance I showed her how to look after the ileostomy. I got into a bit of a mess which was frustrating because I wanted Mum to see how well I was managing. Carol, ever the beacon of positivity explained that it was just a case of being prepared and practice.

Mum was remarkable! If she was shocked by how butchered and sore my tummy looked it never showed, not even for a moment! It must have been horrific for her to see her child's previously perfect skin look so damaged and deformed.

Afterwards when we were having a cup of tea, Mum told me that she was so proud of how I was managing. It was lovely to hear but I wasn't feeling as confident as I was acting. Everyone kept telling me I was doing well and I wanted to believe them. It was difficult because my mood seemed to alter so suddenly. I had been so happy the previous evening and today I felt deflated.

Sensing I was a bit low Mum suggested that she help me wash my hair. It hadn't seen shampoo or conditioner for quite some time and resembled a chip pan. I was a little reluctant to begin with, mainly because the only way to do it was by kneeling over one of the bath tubs. However, with a bit of determined coaxing from Mum I managed to find a position that wasn't too uncomfortable.

Using a jug Mum began pouring water over my hair. Immediately the tension I had been carrying evaporated as the hot water soothed me like a liquid comfort blanket. When she was massaging the shampoo tenderly into my scalp I could have purred like a kitten! It was absolute heaven and quite possibly the greatest suggestion my mum has ever had!

I know she was really grateful to being able to do something nice for me after weeks of having to watch helplessly from the side-lines. While the hair wash itself was immensely blissful, the closeness to Mum was what I really needed. It was the most healing twenty minutes of my entire hospital stay!!

Deep down I knew my mood swings were to be expected. I understood that I had gone through major surgery and would need time to adapt and mend. So despite my impatience, things were progressing in the right direction. I was no longer retching at the sight of the ileostomy which was hugely positive. While I was getting better at changing the bag, unfortunately there were still occasions where I would get in a mess.

One such day I had forgotten to prepare the new bag before taking the old one off. This meant that I needed to cut the flange of the new bag using the template while the ileostomy was uncovered; not ideal but certainly not a calamity. Completely freaking out I hammered on the nurse call bell desperately. By the time Nurse Laura arrived I had worked myself up into a total frenzy! After helping me get the new bag prepared and fitted in place she took my hand. Observing me seriously for a moment she spoke.

'Give yourself a break Jenny. You are expecting too much too soon. Her voice softened, look I know you want to get home but you cannot rush these things!'

Laura's words struck a cord and I realised that I had been putting enormous pressure on myself. I had already overcome so much but for some reason couldn't allow myself to enjoy the triumphs! My impatience was holding me back!

Later that day when I was rooting around in my bedside locker I came across the little china tortoise Nan had given me. She understood my frustrations and in her own quirky way had been trying to tell me to take my time. It was beginning to dawn on me that I didn't have a choice, my body was calling the shots and putting pressure on myself and getting upset was just making everything more difficult.

With a rueful smile I placed the tortoise on top of my locker. For the rest of my hospital stay that was where my dawdling companion remained. It was just an ornament, meaningless to anyone else. For me it held an important and healing message ..... *"Slow and steady wins the race."*

What's Normal Anyway?

I had to admit, once I toned down my expectations it was a lot easier to cope and manage the ileostomy. When the doctors delivered the news that I was finally ready for discharge it took every ounce of my self-control not to streak through the ward with glee!

There is no other way to describe it, going home was fabulous! After nine long weeks as an inpatient I was free. It was a little weird at first; the house seemed tiny after the large open environment of the hospital. Even the walk from the hospital to the car had been an experience. I hadn't been outside for weeks. It felt cold and noisy; almost alien as though I was facing the outside world for the first time.

Not that I was complaining, I was elated to be home! The journey had taken it out of me so I headed up to bed. It was lovely to snuggle under my duvet after the starchy hospital sheets. I sighed contentedly drinking in every inch of my bedroom. It was good to be back in my own space, posters on the walls and books on the shelves. Everything just as I had left it.

Mum came up with a cup of hot chocolate and it struck me; I could have a drink whenever I wanted. No more waiting for the drinks trolley only to be delivered an undrinkable cup of extra strong tea or bitter coffee! I could watch what I wanted on TV. I could have a bath in our family bathroom instead of the communal (and usually smelly) ward washrooms.

Before going into hospital I had taken all of these things for granted. The smallest thing such as using my own pink and white mug felt special. I relished every moment of those first few days home. In a way I had lost some of my identity in hospital becoming more and more institutionalised as I adopted the role of a patient. I left "Jenny" at the door on arrival and collected her on the way out. Unsurprisingly, it was at home my recovery really began.

Carol visited me to check I was coping. I was managing reasonably well but because the ileostomy had shrunk since leaving the hospital the bags weren't fitting correctly. This had caused the contents to leak a couple of times overnight. Carol helped me re measure the ileostomy and created a new template so I could cut the bags to the right size.

'I'm really happy with you dear,' Carol said before adding that she wouldn't need to see me again unless I was worried about anything.

'You have my number, call me if you are struggling or have any questions.'

It sounds ungrateful but I was relieved that I wouldn't be seeing her again anytime soon. Home was my haven, not to be invaded by anyone or anything connected to the hospital. I just wanted to bury all of the pain and trauma of the last few months and bask in the safety and comfort afforded by my family.

Since getting home my appetite had improved dramatically. No longer restricted by the bleak offerings of the hospital kitchen, food was such a novelty. A particular craving I had endured during those long weeks of nil by mouth was for cake.

As a welcome home, Mum baked my favourite carrot cake. My taste buds were reawakened as I devoured the delicately spiced treat. It was utterly delicious; just the right amount of moist in the middle; the outside smothered in gloopy peaks of sickly sweet icing. Given the chance, I probably would have attempted to eat the entire thing myself but Mum had other ideas.

'Do you think you might be ready for visitors?' she said casually, before suggesting I invite a couple of friends from school over for a slice.

We both knew the cake was just an excuse really. In a few weeks' time I would have to face the prospect of returning to school. My crafty (but perceptive) mum was obviously hoping that a visit from my mates would make the transition back a little easier for me.

I asked two girls from my form over. Sharon, Jess and I had been firm friends since the first day of senior school. We had bonded over a mutual appreciation for musical theatre and

Sweet Valley High books! I was giddy with excitement waiting for them to arrive. The doorbell went and I flew down the stairs....

'I'll get it!'

'Alright Jen, grinned Sharon. Where's this cake then?'

Jess flung her arms around me and we were all squealing and talking at once.

Settled in my room with some music playing, they began filling me in on all the changes, new teachers and gossip. We had moved up a year in my absence so there was a lot to discuss. As we were chatting Jess pulled a compact out of her bag. Pouting at her reflection she started to line her eyes with a black kohl eye pencil.

'Since when did you wear makeup?' I teased.

'Everyone wears makeup Jen, she snorted. I'm meeting up with James in a bit,' she added, her cheeks flushing slightly.

'What for?' I asked innocently.

Jess looked at me as though I had grown another head as she expertly smeared some shimmery gloss onto her puckered lips.

'We're seeing each other you dope.'

As Jess and Sharon continued titivating each other I began to realise that a lot had changed since I had last seen them. It had only been a few months but everything seemed different. They were both wearing makeup and perfume. Their clothes were different too, more stylish and sophisticated. My baggy jeans and sweatshirt seemed frumpy in comparison.

The conversation previously consisting of books, school projects and show tunes was now dominated with talk of boys, makeup and fashion. Jess even had a boyfriend!! It was as though someone had skipped forward a vital scene in a movie and I had missed it. That morning I had been so excited about seeing the girls. Now they were here and I couldn't even think of anything to say. I shifted uncomfortably on my bed feeling out of place and strangely lonely. Sharon, now bored of doing her face came and flopped down heavily next to me.

'Look at you Jen, you're a right skinny Minnie,' she remarked, patting my tummy affectionately.

As she touched me her hand brushed lightly over the ileostomy bag and it rustled. Her eyes widened in horror and she pulled away like a scalded cat!

'Oh god, mate I'm really sorry. I didn't mean to touch, well ya know….' she rambled; her voice echoing the shock on her face.

I wanted to tell her it was ok but her intense reaction had stunned me into silence. Fortunately, Mum chose that moment to appear with a tray overflowing with cake and drinks. Sharon and Jess pounced like hyenas on pray, scoffing the goodies in minutes. They were clearly grateful for the distraction.

The conversation drifted back to school life but it was stilted. We were all desperately trying to focus on anything other than the tummy touching incident but it was hanging over us. While the girls were aware that my surgery had resulted in a bag but they had no real comprehension as to what it entailed. I knew Sharon was upset that a moment of affection towards me had caused such tangible awkwardness! They didn't stay for much longer.

'See you when you come back to school Jen,' said Jess as I saw them out.

Sharon was quiet as she hugged me goodbye and I could sense that she was relieved to be going.   The visit hadn't gone as expected. My initial happiness at seeing the girls had diminished and been replaced with a growing despondency. The incident with Sharon was especially playing on my mind. I was angry at myself for being so self-conscious and awkward.

As I obsessed, I found myself wondering if I should've talked to my friends openly about the ileostomy instead of leaving it to the imagination. The problem was that I wouldn't have known where to start! How would I explain to my friends that I now go for a poo via an opening in my tummy into a bag? It was such a personal and delicate subject!

I realised I was frightened of what they would think; how they would look at me. As well as embarrassment in Sharon's face when her hand made contact with the ileostomy, I was sure I had seen a glimmer of something much worse…..disgust. After getting herself a slab of cake she didn't re-join me on the bed, choosing to sit on the floor instead. A rational thinker would have understood this was simply because Sharon was embarrassed and possibly a little upset. My troubled mind interpreted it as something much more distressing. My friend didn't want to sit next to me because the ileostomy repulsed her. I repulsed her!

Within this mixing pot of emotions was anger and resentment. I would have given anything to simply have to deal with usual nuisances of adolescence. Issues like late homework, acne and boys would have been hugely preferable to the worry that a bag containing shit might suddenly leak all over my clothes! Adapting to life with an ileostomy wasn't easy. The changes to my body were so drastic and brutal that trying to stay positive was exhausting. My friends were embracing their teenage years and I was in a completely different place!

These intense feelings of self-consciousness and insecurity were confusing. Every little thing from my clothes to my music selection now seemed immature. Even my beloved books! Up until today I had found the posters of cute puppies and bunnies that decorated my bedroom completely adorable. Now they looked so infantile I wanted to tear them down! Bitter, angry tears flowed as I surrendered to the self-pity.

'Maybe it was a bit too soon for visitors,' said Mum in a futile attempt to pacify me.

This was more than just teenage angst. It was an accumulation of weeks of pain, stress and devastating change. In that moment, I was utterly broken!

The first few weeks following my discharge had been lovely. My family, naturally pleased to have me home had showered me with love and presents. I basked in the attention their relief had spawned but knew the special treatment wouldn't last forever. It was inevitable that Mum and Dad would have to return to work and as time went on daily routines began gradually returning to normal.

With everything I was going through the threat of normality unsettled me. Being wrapped in the familiar warmth of my family gave me a welcome and much needed sense of security. However, I couldn't stay cocooned forever. It was getting harder to hide from the reality of daily life.

I found myself craving the secure uncomplicated atmosphere of the hospital ward which was confusing. All I had done as a patient was beg to be discharged! In the hospital it had been easy. The doctors and nurses weren't intimidated or disturbed by the changes to my body. They had seen it all a hundred times. There had been no need to try and explain what I was dealing with because in the clinical environment it was commonplace.

When I had been in hospital I asked my parents if I could have a puppy. Knowing they would've agreed to almost anything to cheer me up this was slightly manipulative on my part. In order to give me something positive to focus on Mum and Dad gave in and the day we collected Bruno was the happiest I had been for months.

He was a tiny Spaniel with velvet ears and the sweetest baby face. I fell madly in love with him as he snuggled in my arms with a contented sigh. He stayed that way for the entire journey home, occasionally lifting his head to gaze at me with soulful brown eyes. Somehow he knew how much I needed him as my little friend.

Soon inseparable; he followed me around like an adorable shadow. It was good for me to have something other than the ileostomy to centre on and this funny pup was the ideal distraction. He didn't care what I looked like or how I went to the toilet. He even seemed to sense when I was feeling low and would nudge me with his nose demanding attention and making me laugh. His pure and unconditional love was exactly what I needed.

At home I was relaxed. I would laugh at the TV, listen to music and read. Pretty much do all of the things I did before my surgery. Going out was completely different. There was always a slim chance that the ileostomy bag might leak and soil my clothes. If I left the house it was always necessary to carry some essential supplies (spare bag/wipes/fresh underwear/nappy sack) so I could change the bag should the worst happen!

At the very least the bag would need emptying while out and about. The idea of performing either of these tasks in a public toilet made me extremely nervous. So far it was a scenario I had successfully avoided. Aside from short visits to extended family and Bruno's daily dog walk, I barely left the house.

It had been over six weeks since my surgery and I had somehow managed to dodge my friends completely. The awkward couple of hours I had experienced with Sharon and Jess had triggered an unfortunate desire to avoid socialising at all costs. This existence, however "safe" it felt was extremely unhealthy and unfortunately set the precedent for many years of avoidance behaviour.

Although I was happy to hide from the world, the proverbial clock was ticking. Now it was six weeks post-op, the doctors had given me a clean bill of health. So ready or not I was deemed fit enough to return to school. Part of me really wanted to go back. Although I tried to convince myself that I didn't care I was missing my friends. I wanted the regular life of a fourteen year old girl and was sensible enough to know that school would be a good start.

The trouble was I was scared. Returning to classes came with a whole heap of new issues. Having developed quite a knack for finding non-existent problems, my anxiety was like a toxic bath bomb. Instead of infusing bathwater with glorious scent and colour it polluted my thoughts, drowning even the slightest glimmer of optimism!

There was so much to worry about. My classmates were bound to be curious about my lengthy absence. How would I answer the inevitable questions about my surgery? What if the bag leaked or needed changing? How would I catch up with all of the work I had missed? Every time I found a solution to one problem, another appeared. My head pounded as I picked over every possible consequence until I convinced myself that returning to school was impossible.

Obviously my parents weren't as easily sold on the idea that I stay home indefinitely and a meeting was arranged with my head of year. I had never been in trouble at school so sitting outside a teachers office was a first for me.

Mrs Willis had a reputation for being a strict disciplinarian and possessed a low tolerance for bullshit! Even some of the more wilful kids thought twice about trying it on

91

with her. So regardless of the fact I wasn't in trouble, a veil of apprehension cloaked me.

'Stop biting your nails Jen,' scolded Mum pulling my hand away from my mouth.

I threw her a sulky look and sat on my hands. Despite my grouchy attitude I was glad she was with me. At least I wouldn't have to enter the dragon's lair alone! The secretary said that Mrs Willis was ready to see us. Mum knocked on the door and a stern voice rang out.

'Enter!'

The office was bigger than I expected. Dusty pictures adorned the wall and there was a bookcase that went from the floor right up to the ceiling. It was crammed full of books giving the room a cosy library feel.

Sat behind a large and very untidy desk was Mrs Willis. A heavy set woman in her late fifties, she exuded supremacy. Her salt and pepper hair pulled back into a bun so tight it provided a DIY facelift. She had an intense stare, which would have been intimidating had it not been for the comedic amplifying effect of the thick lens glasses balanced on her nose.

Motioning for us to sit down she leaned back in her chair and folded her hands in her lap. Aside from inviting us into her office she hadn't uttered a word. Puzzled by the awkward silence I began to wonder if I was in some sort of trouble; after all I had missed a lot of school. Thankfully at that moment Mrs Willis offered a warm smile.

'Well you have been an extremely brave young lady.'

Her voice, still sharp contradicted the now softer expression on her face. I felt some of the pressure lift. As it turned out, underneath the formidable persona was real kindness and empathy. The compassionate lady in front of me was a stark contrast to her reputation. It wouldn't be an exaggeration to say that she was notorious for reducing even the toughest students to tears.

I never told anyone of the softer side she showed me; intuitively realising her fierce reputation was somehow important in maintaining respect. She was being nice to me so what did I care if the other kids thoughts she was a bitch!

We chatted for a while and she told me I was extremely courageous and that my friends had missed me while I was away. She explained that because I had missed so much school I would be given support to catch up with the work.

'Not that we are worried about getting you up to date Jennifer, we know what a bright girl you are,' she said.

Her positivity was contagious. The icy grip of anxiety which typically accompanied talk of school was fleetingly overshadowed by a glimmer of hope. Could I actually allow myself to believe that everything was going to be alright; maybe even good?

Eventually the conversation turned to my ileostomy. Obviously it was important that I felt comfortable enough to empty and possibly change the bag whilst at school and would need privacy to do so. I only felt truly at ease dealing with the ileostomy at home so this was the aspect of returning to school which worried me the most. As it happened Mrs Willis had been concerned about it too and believed she had the perfect solution.

There was a storage room located next to the girls' cloakroom. It was used by the caretaker to store cleaning materials but it also housed a toilet. The room was always kept locked and I was to have a key. So not only would I have access to my own private toilet I also had somewhere to keep ileostomy supplies and a change of clothes

'That way you won't need to feel embarrassed about any odours when dealing with the bag,' said Mrs Willis.

She was clearly chuffed to have covered all bases and it appeared she had thought of everything. I was a little unsure but grateful none the less. Ready or not everything was set and real life was about to resume. I was going back to school!

May I Be Excused Please?

Despite everyone's efforts and positive attitudes, I had a suspicion that managing at school wasn't going to be so straightforward. However, the big day arrived and for the first time in months I put my uniform on. The blazer felt heavy on my shoulders. I had lost so much weight it completely swamped me. On the plus side it was now big enough to pull over and conceal my tummy. The ileostomy bag wasn't visible by any means but I was still glad of the extra layer.

Typically on a school day, breakfast was a grab a bowl of cereal or slice of toast deal. Today Mum had prepared my absolute favourite, boiled eggs and soldiers; usually devoured in minutes. Not this morning, my stomach lurched at the golden yolk dripping down the side of the egg cup.

'You need to eat something love. You've a long day ahead,' Mum fussed.

Forcing down a piece of toast was like chewing cardboard but I managed and it seemed to appease her. It was time to go and although I was trying my hardest to delay the inevitable, Mum bustled me along. Before I knew it she had bundled me into the car and delivered me to the school gates.

'Have a good day then,' she smiled.

Her chirpy manner didn't quite mask the shadow of worry across her face.

'Yeah, see ya later!'

I also forced my tone to be light hoping to reinforce the illusion of optimism. The truth was that I was painfully nervous!

Some girls from my form were clustered together by the double doors. Unsure of myself I hung back for a moment until Jess saw me and waved.

'Hey Jen! What you doing stood over there you muppet?'

I grinned back at my friend gratefully. The other girls greeted me warmly and despite my nerves it was good to see them. The morning was bitterly cold so even though it was early we trooped inside. This isn't so bad, I thought warming my icy back against the cloakroom radiator. Jess was regaling us with her weekend exploits; the atmosphere was casual and relaxed.....just what I needed! Her story was cut short when the bell rang and we reluctantly headed to the classroom.

The first two periods were double maths with Mr Ramack. Not exactly a thrilling start to the day. However, the level of concentration required to plough through the long multiplication was a blessing in disguise. Everyone was so absorbed in their work that I was able to slip elusively back into class without a fuss. My plan was to fly under the radar until the novelty of my return subsided. The last thing I needed was to be singled out and bombarded with awkward questions.

It was towards the end of the lesson when Mr Ramack began to discuss our upcoming coursework projects. A dull man, who could turn the most interesting topic into a snore fest, had no chance of making maths coursework sound appealing. As his monotonous voice droned on he appeared unaware that no one was listening. Half of the class were fidgeting restlessly while the remainder drooped in their seats like depressed, wilting flowers.

The sound of the bell cut through the tedious atmosphere and created a burst of energy so instant it was almost Pavlovian.

'Don't forget you are due to hand in your proposals next Monday. NO EXCUSES,' the hapless teacher shouted over the chatter and frantic bag packing!

The class charged out of the room anxious not to miss a moment of glorious break time! I had almost made it out of the door when Mr Ramack beckoned me over.

'It's nice to see you Jenny! When you are settled we will need to get you up to speed!'

My heart sank a little but I nodded and thanked him, trying to match his enthusiasm.

'A bit of hard work and you will be back on track, no problem.' he continued.

Unsure how to respond, I glanced longingly at the door. All I wanted was to survive the first day with no major mishaps. Everything else could wait! Perhaps detecting my discomfort or ready for his mid-morning caffeine fix, Mr Ramack dismissed me and I gladly escaped. Jess was waiting outside scuffing her foot impatiently.

'C'mon Jen, there won't be any sausage rolls left,' she moaned linking my arm to hurry me along.

Sausage rolls were the last thing on my mind as we reached the cafeteria. It was quarter to eleven and I hadn't emptied the ileostomy bag since first thing. Mumbling to Jess that I was going to the loo I hastily broke away from my friends as they queued for snacks.

Mercifully none of them wanted to join me to pay a visit! I hadn't told anyone I would be using a separate toilet. It just sounded weird and would lead to endless questions. Questions I didn't quite know how to answer!

I stood outside the toilet and fumbled in my bag for the key. There were quite a few other students milling around and I was anxious not to draw attention to myself. Managing to furtively unlock the door and slip inside I let out a sigh of relief.

There was a box of ileostomy supplies on a little shelf which Mum had left for me just in case I needed to change the bag. Right now it just needed emptying so I deftly unclipped the end and evacuated the contents into the loo. Fastening the clip securely back in place to prevent the bag from leaking I tucked everything inside my underwear and did up my trousers. The deed was done.

It was always so smelly when I emptied the bag; it still made me heave at times. Suddenly paranoid that the smell would linger on me, I washed my hands twice and liberally sprayed myself with perfume.

Just as I was leaving I caught a glimpse of myself in a small mirror on the wall. My face was pinched and I was clenching my jaw tensely. I looked so tightly wound, it was pitiful. How was it possible that a task as simple as visiting the toilet could make me feel so jittery? After splashing some cold water on my face I exited the room quickly and went to find my mates.

The bell ringing for third period echoed through the corridor. I hadn't even managed to get a drink so had to settle for a swift glug from the water fountain before trudging along to the next lesson. The buoyancy of surviving the morning's classes had now been replaced with heaviness. Using the private toilet had put me on edge. How would I explain if someone asked me what was in the room and why I had a key? My heart had been pounding as I slipped in and out of the toilet; like an undercover agent desperate not to attract attention.

Hating myself for being so pathetic I tried to concentrate on my French verbs. It didn't work. No matter how much I tried not to worry, I was already dreading the next time I needed to use the toilet. This was one of many difficulties I faced whilst trying to integrate back into school. There was absolutely no question that I would have struggled to use the communal toilets, mainly because of the repugnant odour released when emptying the bag. I was a self-conscious fourteen year old, so unleashing a shitty smell in my peers' lavatories would have been the ultimate humiliation.

Having my own "special" toilet was certainly the lesser of two evils but resulted in terrible anxiety none the less. I would lurk near the door, my eyes darting around willing people to disappear so I could slither in unnoticed. Exiting the toilet was even more stressful; listening at the door and waiting for silence before daring to move.

Of course in reality no one was paying the slightest bit of attention. The teachers were aware of my situation and the other students were more concerned with their own issues. They had better things to do than spend time monitoring my daily movements. As usual, the rational side of my brain was smothered by anxiety. Slowly but surely the phobia took hold and grew. On a bad day, the sight of the toilet key nestled between my school books was all it would take to induce panic!

With ever increasing stress levels, the last thing I needed was another embarrassing problem to contend with. Unfortunately, life with an ileostomy brings with it many challenges. One in particular was so mortifying that functioning daily became a living hell!

An ileostomy works of its own accord, expelling waste into the bag intermittently. It is completely different to emptying your bowels "normally" through the anus. A healthy individual senses the urge to open their bowels and will do so at a convenient moment. There is no such control with an ileostomy it is simply active when it needs to be. So all I could do was empty the attached bag once full.

As well as the usual waste, wind is also released via the ileostomy; something which wouldn't have been a major issue….had it not been for the noise! Imagine the embarrassment of letting off uncontrollable farts during a silent study period in the library.

I was trying so hard to settle back into school. It wasn't enough that every day was a battle against increasing and crippling anxiety. Now I had to endure the embarrassment of rude noises randomly exploding from my person. Sod's law the ileostomy always seemed to be more active during the quietest lessons. I would press my hands over it in a frantic attempt to muffle the hideous spluttering while some smart arse would yell out,

'Who just farted?'

My furious blushes making it glaringly obvious that I was the stinky culprit. The shame radiated from me like a neon arrow flashing above my head! Every day was an embarrassing nightmare on a loop. Had I been older and more secure in myself then maybe I would have coped with it but after everything I had already been through it was just too much.

Carol had promised that nobody would know I had an ileostomy unless I chose to tell them. It seemed this disgusting "thing" on my tummy had other ideas and wanted the world to know of its' existence! I felt mislead, ashamed and bitterly angry. It was a struggle to accept such massive image changes on a private level. The inability to conceal these changes from my classmates was making this acceptance impossible to achieve. My body was betraying me yet again and I was losing the will to fight.

This issue became so severe that Mum took me to see Carol to discuss it. She tried to tell me that the noise sounded worse to me because I was so sensitive to it. Bullshit!

'It's really noisy, people notice,' I pleaded, desperate for her to understand how mortifying it was.

Carol had a few suggestions to help reduce the amount of wind I produced. These included eating live yoghurts, taking charcoal tablets and drinking peppermint tea. She also gave me a list of foods that created wind so I would know which to avoid and advised me to eat little and often.

I went away determined that these suggestions would lessen these embarrassing noises and religiously avoided any foods notorious for wind production. I stuck to eating things that did the opposite such at the live yoghurts which, despite my scepticism were surprisingly effective. In fact, they worked so well I became quite fixated, forcing myself to eat five pots throughout the day and vehemently refusing to go to school if I was missing even one.

Of course, it wasn't really about the yoghurts and I certainly didn't need to consume so many. It was a control issue. There had been so many times since my diagnosis of UC when I hadn't felt in charge of my body, my health, even my life! As well as this I had the further pressures of being a teen, trying to fit in at school and catch up with all of the work I had missed.

This wasn't the normality I had anticipated following the surgery. My expectations had been clouded and unrealistic. Of course it was wonderful to no longer have the debilitating symptoms of UC to contend with but I hadn't envisioned life with an ileostomy would be quite so difficult.

While my diet had tamed the embarrassing noises it didn't completely prevent the ileostomy from releasing gas. If I didn't get to the toilet regularly to deflate the bag then it would fill up so tightly I was terrified it might explode. Not only that but when full of wind the bulge under my clothes was clearly visible (at least it was to me).

It would have been more than adequate to empty the bag every couple of hours, however my obsessive need for control caused me to do it every twenty minutes. I could only relax if the bag was completely flat against my tummy.

My paranoia became so great that even when the bag was empty I believed it was visible. I began untucking my school shirt to create a baggy layer over my tummy. The school uniform policy was quite strict so Mum wrote me a note explaining that I had permission to wear my shirt untucked.

As the majority of my teachers were aware of my circumstances, getting reprimanded for wearing my uniform incorrectly was unlikely. However, in my tormented state there were potential problems and embarrassments lurking everywhere. A bundle of nervous energy, I was as jumpy as the proverbial cat on hot bricks.

Predictably my school work began to suffer. I was already over six months behind so this was far from ideal! It seemed impossible to concentrate on anything other than the ileostomy. My academic struggles were noticed by my concerned teachers and it was suggested that I should repeat the school year. At the very least this would eliminate the pressures associated with playing catch up.

Most kids would be distraught at the prospect of moving down a year and leaving their friends. I couldn't have cared less, living only for the approaching summer break. No school or stress for six blissful weeks! I would worry about the new term in September, until then I was free!

The holidays were hot and sticky. Opening a window let in the soundtrack of children running through sprinklers; squealing with delight as the icy jets pelted them. The bright days and smells of summer were uplifting and everyone seemed happier.

Not faced with school I had relaxed considerable, it was as though a weight had been temporarily lifted. Content to stay at home I spent my time reading in the garden. It was peaceful to escape into a world beyond my own, surrounded by characters so familiar they were like friends.

Once or twice I went into town with Sharon to look around the shops but this dwindled out. Sharon had got a steady boyfriend and we had begun to drift apart anyway. I couldn't imagine ever wanting a boyfriend. I was too socially anxious to spend time with my close girlfriends let alone be intimate with a boy. My body repulsed me so it was only logical to assume that others would feel the same.

All of my friends were growing up and maturing, leaving me behind. Even though I was isolated and lonely, those feelings were preferable to the anxiety that accompanied any form of social contact. As I withdrew more and more, Mum urged me to have friends over and get involved in fun activities but I wasn't interested. The only other person I felt truly comfortable was Nan.

'You should be out with your friends Jen, not spending all your time with an old crow like me,' she would say not realising that her words made me feel even more of a freak.

I knew it wasn't healthy or normal for a girl of my age to hide away but the alternative was too much to bear. We went on our annual family holiday to Dorset. I had been looking forward to it but watching the gangs of teenagers hanging round the arcades and burger bar made me miserable. I resented them for having fun and for being so carefree and detested myself for being such an oddity.

Small Steps and Triumphs

The new school year began and despite dropping down a year nothing improved. I had never really resolved my difficulties, simply placed them in a mental filing cabinet to be dealt with later. Once faced with reality, it soon became evident that my problems were insurmountable!

In school I felt stifled and trapped with anxiety levels so high my body was in a constant state of fight or flight. An intense desire to escape was a dominant and exhausting feature of each day. I would find myself hiding in the toilet choking back tears while desperately cooking up ways to be sent home.

The yoghurts to help control the wind explosions were making me feel sick which was hardly surprising given the quantity I was eating! Even so I was unable to go anywhere or do anything without forcing them down. They still turn my stomach to this day!

I was falling apart mentally, constantly frustrated and angry with myself for being so weak. I would lie in bed at night and angrily thump at the ileostomy as if I was trying to push it back into the inside of my body where it belonged. My body image and self-perception were so badly damaged that I detested the very thing that had saved my life.

Every single morning my parents would have a huge battle on their hands as I would plead not to have to go to school. On particularly bad days becoming so hysterical I would be physically sick. Nothing could persuade me to leave the house. Mum and Dad tried to be firm but seeing me so distraught meant they didn't have the heart to force the issue. It was a waste of time anyway; on the odd occasion they got me to school I would be in the nurses' office by nine thirty crying to go home.

I don't think anyone knew what to do for the best. One teacher even commented that the school weren't equipped to deal with my "problems" and that I should be asked to leave.

This really upset my parents. They knew that I wasn't being intentionally difficult and that my struggles were genuine, they just didn't know how to help me.

It soon became clear that the battle to get me to attend school wasn't going to be won. I knew that my behaviour was making life difficult for everyone and this filled me with shame. The trouble was I had completely shut down and couldn't seem to function.

There were official meetings and serious conversations between the adults. I had a visit from some education officials who asked a lot of questions. It was scary as I didn't want my parents to be penalised for not getting me to school. Finally it was agreed that school wasn't the correct environment for me. I had developed too many problems and it was distressing for everyone; not to mention distracting for the other students every time I had a meltdown. My future seemed bleak and depressing but Mum refused to let me sink.

'There is never a problem we can't solve! We will figure something out Jen,' she would say in her upbeat positive way.

They say you should always listen to your mother! Just when I was at my lowest ebb we received a phone call from a local college. The school had contacted them to explain my situation and see if they could offer a solution. The relief I experienced when they suggested I join their flexible learning scheme was immense! The course would enable me to work towards my exams at home and couldn't have been more perfect! For the first time in months I experienced something I thought was lost forever.....it was hope!

The college course was great. I had to meet up with my personal tutor once a week for an hour. I would hand in my work and we would go over my previous assignments. There were occasions where going to the weekly meetings would generate some anxiety but it was nothing compared to the level of attending school. What was expected of me now was manageable and that made all the difference.

While college allowed me to continue with my education my confidence levels and self-esteem were still low. I was living in my own little world and aside from short trips to college or a visit to Nans' I barely left the house. I would struggle even to mix with my extended family seeming like a freak compared to my cousins who were all popular and doing well at school.

I viewed myself as a failure, a school dropout and I would project these negative emotions onto my family. Of course they were all just sorry I was having such a tough time and didn't think badly of me. Sadly, negative thinking was my favourite go to response. I would habitually put myself down for finding life so difficult post-surgery instead of allowing myself to enjoy each effort and success.

Everyone has that inner voice which in a balanced mind is usually a helpful tool; existing to offer constructive criticism and growth. Mine had evolved into a spiteful bully! It was a powerful force, skulking in the corners of my mind waiting to pounce should I dare to feel positive. If I could pen a letter to my fifteen year old self it would begin with.....

"Dear Jen,
For the love of god, give yourself a break!!!"

I successfully passed two exams following the flexible study program which amazed me and was a much needed boost. With Mum and Dads' encouragement and some intensive counselling sessions I decided to enrol at the college to take three more GCSEs.

It was a step up from the flexible program meaning I would actually have to attend classes for two hours each day. The college, aware of my difficulties were extremely supportive. None the less this was going to be a massive trial. As comfortable as I had grown, existing in an impenetrable bubble at home, this had only reinforced my avoidance behaviour. However passing the first two exams had given me a taste of success and I really wanted to try.

The anxiety attacks resurfaced and brought with them the obsessive yogurt consumption before every class. My GP suggested I try the complementary therapy, Rescue Remedy as an aid to lower my stress levels. It definitely had a calming effect which was great but similar to my reliance on the yoghurts, I became slightly fixated. There was always a bottle of this soothing potion burrowed in my coat pocket. I didn't necessarily need it but just knowing it was there reassured me, my herbal security blanket.

Surprisingly, I found myself enjoying college life and worked hard. It was great to focus on something other than the ileostomy. As I only had to get through a couple of hours a day, emptying the bag was not the problem it had been at school. It could usually wait until I got home which meant there was no need for a private toilet!

The leap from studying at home to attending a few classes might have seemed insignificant but it was a huge undertaking for me. Every lesson I successfully sat through without a panic attack forcing me to flee, was an achievement. There were cracks appearing in the wall of self-doubt I had built around me. Given, these cracks were so minute they were barely visible....but they were there all the same!

I made friends with Clare, a shy girl in my class. Although we didn't socialise outside of college it was nice to make a connection of sorts. Sometimes we would go for a milkshake in the café between classes which, to begin with made me panic. Old habits and months of isolation will do that to a person!

Clare knew nothing of my health problems which helped. It was as though the slate had been wiped clean, a fresh start. Suddenly I wasn't just a girl whose life was defined by an ileostomy, (although I still greatly resented its existence). Now that good things were happening too; the bad didn't seem quite so......well bad!

Making friends wasn't my main priority. Aside from Clare I didn't mix, choosing to throw myself into assignments instead. It was an area of my life I had control over and working hard paid dividend. I regularly received high praise from my college tutors and the positive feedback was like a drug; I just wanted more and more.

My good grades were a pin prick of light emerging through the persistent grey clouds. I had been so down for so long that now, even the simplest of gesture would give me an enormous high. An encouraging smile from a tutor, or a nod of approval when I contributed in class was enough to leave me soaring for days! If that was all it took to make me happy, imagine the joy when not only did I survive sitting the final exams…… but also managed to achieve straight A's! The highest grades in my class! Mum and I were dancing around the living room waving my results letter in the air as if it were the Nobel Prize!

Wanting more I decided to enrol onto a BTEC National Diploma in Health Studies for the following September. My fascination with the human body and love of science naturally propelled me towards this subject. It was an exciting but colossal step. Up until now I had taken things very slowly. The transition from studying at home to attending a couple of daily classes had only gone smoothly because of this!

The BTEC was a full time course which meant a nine till five commitment. It would be a leap but I was certain that I could do it. This sudden spike in self-belief wasn't simply down to my academic success. By the time the new course began, the most challenging aspect of my life would be over. I was now seventeen and considered physically developed enough to be considered for the surgery to reverse the ileostomy.

Knowing my tendency to rush in blindly, Mum tentatively suggested I would need more information before making any final decisions.

'There isn't anything to decide! I don't care what's involved, I want to go ahead,' I said stubbornly.

Yes, I had forged an existence of sorts but life with an ileostomy had never been a long term plan. The only thing that had got me out of bed some mornings was the knowledge that the bag wasn't necessarily a permanent fixture……that one day it would be gone and my life might return to some semblance of normal!

'Just don't get your hopes up or expect too much, urged Mum. We need to talk it all through with the consultant; it might not even be an option for you.'

'Don't say that,' I snapped.

Mum sighed wearily at my predictable reaction. The mere suggestion that the surgery may not be viable obviously triggered some strong emotions.

'I'm sure it will be I just don't want you to be disappointed. Let's wait and see eh?'

I knew that Mum was right and this irritated me. My high hopes about the previous surgery had led to me being crushed when the reality didn't match my expectations. The sensible approach was to wait and not make any decisions until we had all the facts. This was easier said than done! Caution was the enemy as it presented the possibility of a future I simply didn't want to envisage!

Life with a permanent ileostomy was so abhorrent, so incomprehensible to me that denial was my only defence. Any attempts to keep an open mind were futile; nothing could dull my certainty. The reversal surgery was going to be a success! I was going to be normal again! What's more, it couldn't happen soon enough!

Mr Mills

The consultant who would perform my surgery was one of the leading surgeons in his field. Mr Mills was unlike any other consultant I had encountered. He carried a sort of mad professor vibe with dishevelled hair and crazy eyebrows.

His trousers, slightly short would rise up when he sat down to reveal colourful and mismatched socks. He always wore a blue corduroy suit teamed with a red polka dot bow tie. The only time I ever saw him without his distinctive neck wear was when he was in theatre scrubs.

It is hard to explain, but even wearing the generic scrubs he stood out, a quirky charm just emanated from him. His lilting Irish accent was so melodic and gentle it had a soothing quality. When he spoke everything was calm.

The first time I met Mr Mills was to discuss the potential surgery and my parents were with me. He silently entered the consultation room and before uttering a word to anyone he did something none of my other doctors had done. He moved his chair from behind the desk to beside mine, sat down and shook my hand warmly. Consultants are highly skilled and the work they do is both brilliant and awe inspiring. This excellence can at times be shrouded by a veil of power and intimidation. The informal act of sitting next to me rather than behind a desk instantly put us on the same level.

Mr Mills was warm and open and *always* spoke directly to me rather than above me or through my parents. Again these may seem like insignificant details but each one made a huge difference to how I felt and responded. He was the first consultant to ever treat me as an adult and with absolute respect and honesty; how I felt genuinely mattered to him. The respect was mutual and I completely trusted him; he made me feel safe.

I have been treated by numerous medical professionals over the years. The majority of whom could pass me in the street and I wouldn't recognise them. They are just faceless memories.

I remember every little detail about Mr Mills from our first meeting to the last. This is not simply because he was quirky and funny but because he was *kind*!

It was imperative I had all of the necessary information about the proposed surgery in order to make an informed decision. As Mr Mills began to talk me through it all he adopted a more serious stance. The jovial doctor became solemn to the point of stern; colours he didn't wear well but necessary none the less. He spoke with complete candour about what I would be undertaking and made it clear that it wasn't going to be easy. By the end of the consultation I was under no illusions; this wasn't going to be a quick fix, or by any means a perfect alternative to having an ileostomy! Mr Mills implored me to understand what was involved.

'Your bowels will never function in the usual way. It just isn't going to happen, even after this surgery. That is a fact you need to process and accept.'

He emphasized that while pouch surgery was certainly a good option for me I should consider it carefully as it wasn't without its own issues.

'You will have to learn to live with a pouch and initially you will be visiting the toilet multiple times a day and probably at night too. You will pass only loose stools for the lifetime of the pouch so essentially you will always have diarrhoea. Once your muscles improve we would hope that you will be able to control your bowels but you may experience some incontinence.'

Sensing my deflation the doctor took my hand again.

'I know some of what I have said isn't what you want to hear Jenny. It would be wrong of me to tell you that living with a pouch is easy. It isn't, but for many it is preferable to the ileostomy. The lesser of two evils if you will! Something tells me you are a determined young woman!'

He winked to convey that my resolve hadn't gone unnoticed.

I went home with a library of leaflets. Mr Mills wanted me to read, digest and discuss it all with my parents. Ever the dutiful patient, I trawled through the literature taking on board every aspect, positive and negative! The information regarding the downsides to pouch surgery made little impact. Nothing could have convinced me not to go ahead. Mr Mills suggested that I should undergo a couple of counselling sessions to help me decide; but even the miniscule risk of someone putting doubts in my head ruled out that idea!

No, I refused to allow anyone to influence me. My stubborn mind simply couldn't (or perhaps wouldn't) visualise a happy fulfilling life with an ileostomy. It had caused me so much anguish and embarrassment that I was simply unable to move beyond those feelings.

How could I ever accept or make peace with something that repelled me so intensely? Irrational as it was, I honestly believed the ileostomy was the root cause of every single problem. Hell, a spot could appear on my face and somehow the ileostomy was responsible. Over time this blinkered view had grown into an unrealistic but deep-seated belief......that by eliminating the ileostomy, all of my problems would miraculously disappear.

Mr Mills had stressed the importance of preparing for the chance that the pouch surgery may fail. The only outcome in this case would be a permanent ileostomy; a fact which filled me with anxiety. My go to defence mechanism was denial. Every time the thought of surgery failure buzzed around my head like a bothersome gnat, I swatted it away and focused on something else!

The way I saw it, this surgery was my one and only chance. It was being offered to me and I would be doing myself a wrong if I didn't try. Even if managing with a pouch turned out to be difficult I convinced myself that it couldn't be any worse than having an ileostomy.

I had fantasized about being ileostomy free for such a long time. The anticipation of it becoming a reality was intense! My hopes were high with every imagined outcome transforming my life for the better.

I wanted my intestines to be back on the inside of my body where they belonged; to run my hands down my tummy only to feel smooth, unbroken skin. I wanted to wear tight clothes without having to worry about the bag filling with wind and becoming visible to the world. To be able to leave the house without supplies and spare clothes in case the bag should leak. I wanted to be able to sit comfortably with my friends and not be plagued by the worry of sudden embarrassing noises. *I just wanted to be free!*

Mr Mills had insisted that I should try to reach my final decision based on fact rather than emotion. At the time I agreed but really I was just paying lip service. It was unfair and unrealistic to expect me to use the logical side of my brain to decide on something I was so emotionally invested in.

So while I did read all of the literature regarding the surgery; I was just going through the motions and nodding in all the right places. It was more a case of "when" than "if" because for me, the die was cast; it had been for a very long time!

Time Heals All Wounds?

This was twenty years ago and thankfully the surgery was a complete success. It sounds strange but for some reason I never doubted it would be. It was almost as though my unfaltering certainty made it so. I remember looking down at my tummy afterwards and sobbing. It was a painful map of angry wounds and stitches, but all I felt was overwhelming relief because the ileostomy had gone.

The first time I sat on the toilet to evacuate my bowels was an odd experience. I was a little scared to push as I was very sore but also because I hadn't pooed through my bottom in over three years! It was a peculiar yet reassuringly familiar sensation.

I couldn't help but laugh at the absurdity of my feelings. Most people experience delight at the birth of a child or passing their driving test. Here I was perched on the loo, positively ecstatic because I was crapping through the hole in my backside!

So....did the fact I no longer had an ileostomy instantly make life wonderful? Of course it didn't! Over the three years it existed I had blamed the ileostomy for most, if not all of my problems. It was easier to do that than it was to face my fears and fight!

I had known that I should be thankful. That without the surgery to remove my diseased bowel and create the ileostomy I almost certainly would have died. To try and feel gratitude towards something you loathe is deeply conflicting. It would be difficult for a person of emotional maturity to negotiate such muddled feelings; so at fourteen it was quite beyond me. As I look back and reflect it is easier to appreciate how fortunate I was. Or perhaps I have simply developed a quiet respect now it is all just a memory.

Life with an Ileo-anal pouch comes with its' own set of unique challenges. For the first few months post-surgery I was emptying the pouch between fifteen to twenty times daily. This has improved to a more manageable level over time. Unless I am unwell, I will usually visit the toilet ten times a day and twice overnight.

There are occasions when the pouch can be unpredictable, for example when suffering a bout of pouchitis (inflammation of the pouch). So to avoid any embarrassing accidents I tend to stay home during these "risky" periods.

Overnight trips with friends are awkward and personally one of the more problematic features of pouch life. This is due to the fact that the pouch is extremely explosive; therefore emptying it is noisy and messy. Using a public or a friends' toilet can be embarrassing to say the least! During the first few years post-surgery there were occasions when I made myself unwell by holding on until I got home.

There are a few tricks I have picked up over the years. When using a public toilet I try to wait until someone uses the hand dryer before exploding. Alternatively, a well-timed flush of the toilet can drown out some of the noise!

As was the case with the ileostomy, certain wind producing foods are best avoided and if I am going to be out for the day peppermint tea is my saviour. As effective as they are, I draw the line at live yoghurt. I have eaten more than my share of that over the years and quite frankly would rather fart up a storm!

Now I am older, the noises and smells don't worry me quite as much. Yes, it's embarrassing but everyone has to poo and everyone farts. Mine are just slightly more impressive that's all!

The hardest part of recovering has been mentally. My early experiences with IBD left not only physical but lasting emotional scars. The continuous struggles I have faced with anxiety and OCD were probably unavoidable. I have also suffered periods of severe and debilitating depression. It would be naïve to think that a person could endure such trauma at a tender age and come out unscathed. It isn't self-pity or weakness; it's just the way it is!

Anyone who suffers with mental illness will face a battle unique to them and no two experiences will ever be the same. I am prescribed anti-depressants and have been since my early twenties. The medication has most definitely made a difference to my well-being. I have discovered it is much more effective when used alongside other techniques.

I draw on mindfulness meditation and positive imagery a great deal and find them to be extremely enriching practices. There is a lot to be said for living in the moment, focusing on what is happening right here, right now!

It has taken many sessions of Cognitive Behaviour Therapy to learn the techniques to manage my anxiety and depression effectively. I recognise that in order to stay healthy I need to care about myself and invest time. It isn't easy and I don't imagine it ever will be but once I began to achieve acceptance and balance, things gradually became more manageable.

Recently I realised that I was gaining control over these destructive mental illnesses and this was leading to positive changes in my attitude, behaviour and ultimately my life. Self-awareness is a great tool and used correctly leads to empowerment and strength.

Learning and utilising relaxation techniques can be valuable for everyone, regardless of mental health status. Mindfulness in particular can have positive implications for those who have busy lives and busy minds. It is even possible to peel a potato mindfully and take yourself out of your own headspace for a while!

I was very sceptical when these techniques were first introduced to me and genuinely didn't think they would make any difference. They take practice and patience but I would highly recommend that those looking to quieten down any chaos within to give them a try. You have absolutely nothing to lose and everything to gain!

The unpredictability of my physical and mental health has made it incredibly hard for me to hold down a job. There are not many employers who take kindly to a member of their staff needing multiple days off throughout the year. This is something I have struggled to accept. Numerous absences and unreliability have led to me leaving many jobs.

I hated myself for letting people down and this has at times, fuelled my depression. I used to worry that I would be perceived as lazy, which isn't the case; I'm actually extremely conscientious and hard-working. As I have got older I have learnt to be kinder to myself and to accept my limitations. I'm not suggesting that the pouch has held me back; it's just that certain aspects of life are slightly more difficult for me and need to be approached differently.

While I like to push myself I always try to direct my energy into things I know are achievable without causing unnecessary stress. For example, I work from home now which means I am able to challenge myself and have positive goals to focus on. Also ideal for the days I'm unwell and need to stay near the toilet! My life isn't conventional but this doesn't mean that I am not a valuable and functioning member of society.

Life isn't black and white. It's a kaleidoscope of colours, tests of strength and faith alongside moments of absolute joy and exhilaration – and it is like that for every single one of us! The most important lesson I have learned over the years is to never give up!

I have achieved things I would never have dreamed possible as that terrified fourteen year old crying in a school toilet. I graduated from University with First Class Honours. A love of musical theatre prompted me to join a choir and I even found the courage to sing a solo at The Birmingham Symphony Hall in front of two thousand people! Utterly terrifying but so exciting!

My beloved Nan passed away after a battle with dementia. I was lucky enough to help care for her during those last few years and we shared some truly precious times together. She is always with me, all I have to do is look at that little china tortoise and I can hear her saying

'Slow and steady Jen, that's the way.'

Of all the good times I have had, the pivotal and most life changing was falling in love. My husband is kind, funny and incredibly supportive. I am so comfortable with him I never need to worry about making noises or smells on the toilet. He doesn't care about the ugly scars I have been left with and looks after me on the days I am not so well. It is a truly remarkable feeling to know that someone accepts and loves you unconditionally. The day we got married on a beach in Cyprus surrounded by our families was the happiest I have ever been. I was where I wanted to be and nothing else mattered.

While it was never my intention to share my journey with IBD as a form of self-therapy it has been unexpectedly cathartic. I see myself with new and gentler eyes. Instead of focusing on the struggles I have faced because of the IBD I now appreciate everything I have achieved *in spite* of it! I have so much empathy and compassion for anyone who is ill or suffering (and that includes me).

It is so important to appreciate every single day, good or bad. The bad ones just make the good that little bit more blissful. Whatever the circumstances, I will never stop striving to achieve the best life possible! Why would I? I've made it this far....

Two Wolves

    'An old Cherokee is teaching his grandson about life. "A fight is going on inside me" he said to the boy. "It is a terrible fight and it is between two wolves. One is evil – he is fear, anger, sorrow, regret, greed, arrogance, self-pity, guilt, resentment, superiority, lies, false pride, inferiority and ego" He continued, "The other is good – he is joy, peace, love, hope, serenity, humility, kindness, benevolence, empathy, generosity, truth, compassion and faith. The same fight is going on inside you – and inside every other person too." The grandson thought about it for a minute and then asked his grandfather, "Which wolf will win?"

    The old Cherokee simply replied, "The one you feed".

Further Information

Ulcerative Colitis (UC) and Crohn's disease are the two main forms of Inflammatory Bowel Disease (IBD)

The digestive system is a group of organs working together to convert food into energy and basic nutrients to feed the entire body. Food passes through a long tube inside the body known as the alimentary canal or **the gastrointestinal** tract (GI tract).

Ulcerative Colitis is a chronic condition that causes inflammation and ulceration of the inner lining of the rectum and colon (the large bowel). In UC, tiny ulcers develop on the surface of the lining and these may bleed and produce pus.

Crohn's Disease is a chronic condition that causes inflammation of the digestive system (also known as the gastrointestinal tract or gut). Crohn's causes ulceration and inflammation that affects the body's ability to digest food, absorb nutrients and eliminate waste in a healthy way.
UC and Crohn's disease are chronic conditions. This means that they are continuous and life-long. However there may be long periods of good health (remission), along with times when the symptoms are more active (relapses or flare-ups).

It is believed that IBD is triggered or brought on by certain factors.
Genetic makeup
An irregular reaction of the immune system (autoimmune response) to particular bacteria in the intestines probably initiated by something in the environment.

Possible environmental triggers of IBD
Viruses
Bacteria

Diet

Stress

Smoking is another possible environmental trigger in Crohn's disease.

There is no definite evidence that any one of these things is responsible for causing IBD.

Differences between UC and Crohn's disease

Difference	Ulcerative Colitis	Crohn's Disease
Location	Large intestine (Colon) is typically the only affected site.	Inflammation may occur anywhere along the digestive tract.
Inflammation	Inflammation is continuous throughout the affected area.	Inflammation may occur in patches
Pain	Pain is common in the lower left part of the abdomen.	Pain is commonly experienced in the lower right abdomen.
Appearance	Colon wall is thicker and shows continuous inflammation. Mucus lining of the large intestine may have ulcers but they do not extend beyond the inner lining.	Colon wall may be thickened and have a rocky appearance. Ulcers along the digestive tract are deep and may extend into all layers of the bowel wall.
Bleeding	Bleeding from the rectum during bowel movements.	Bleeding from the rectum during bowel movements is uncommon.

Columbia St Mary's http://www.columbia-stmarys.org/Crohn_vs_Ulcerative_Colitis

Symptoms of Ulcerative Colitis (UC)	Symptoms of Crohn's Disease
Abdominal pain or discomfort	Abdominal pain, cramping or
Anaemia caused by severe bleeding	swelling
Bloody diarrhoea	Anaemia
Dehydration	Fever
Fatigue	Gastrointestinal bleeding
Fever	Joint pain
Joint pain	Malabsorption
Loss of appetite	Persistent or recurrent diarrhoea
Malabsorption	Stomach ulcers
Rectal bleeding	Vomiting
Urgent bowel movements	Weight loss
Weight loss	

Columbia St Mary's http://www.columbia-stmarys.org/Crohn_vs_Ulcerative_Colitis

TYPES OF ULCERATIVE COLITIS

Ulcerative Colitis is generally categorised according to how much of the colon is affected.

Proctitis
In proctitis only the rectum is inflamed. This means that the rest of the colon is healthy and can still function normally.

Left-sided (or Distal) Colitis
In this type of UC the inflammation starts at the rectum and continues up the left side of the colon (also known as the distal or descending colon)

Extensive and Total Colitis
Extensive colitis extends along most of the colon.
For further and more detailed information about types of UC please see the Crohn's and Colitis UK booklet 'Ulcerative Colitis'

TYPES OF CROHN'S DISEASE

Terminal ileal and ileocecal

Crohn's in the ileum (the last part of the small intestine) may be called ileal or sometimes 'terminal ileal' Crohn's – because it is affecting the terminus or end of the ileum. If it also affects the beginning of the large bowel it is known as ileocecal Crohn's

Small bowel

Abdominal pain and diarrhoea are also common symptoms of Crohn's further up the small bowel.

Colonic

Crohn's Disease in the colon (large intestine or large bowel) is often called Crohn's Colitis. This is also a common form of Crohn's disease.

Gastroduodenal

Crohn's in the upper gut – the oesophagus, stomach or duodenum – is much less common.

Perianal

Crohn's in the area around the anus (back passage) can occur on its own or at the same time as inflammation in other parts of the body. Symptoms include:
• Fissures – these are tears in the lining of the anal canal
• Skin tags – small fleshy growths around the anus.
• Haemorrhoids – swollen areas in the anal canal.
• Abscesses – collections of pus that can become swollen and painful.
• Fistulas – these are narrow tunnels or passageways between the gut and the skin or another organ.

Oral Crohn's

Crohn's can occasionally affect the mouth.

Complications of Crohn's disease can occur and these may be in the gut or elsewhere in the body. Examples of complications in the gut are strictures, perforations and fistulas.

For further and more detailed information about Crohn's disease please see the Crohn's and Colitis UK leaflet 'Crohn's Disease.

IBD AND BOWEL CANCER

IBD isn't a form of cancer. However there is an increased risk of developing cancer if there has been severe and extensive disease for 8-10 years from when symptoms began. If this is the case then it is advisable to have surveillance tests/procedures to monitor for changes in the bowel or cancer. *For further and more detailed information in this area please see the Crohn's and Colitis UK Information sheet 'Bowel cancer and IBD'*

DIAGNOSIS OF IBD

Blood and Stool Tests
Simple blood tests can show if there is inflammation somewhere in the body and if a person is anaemic. Stool can also be tested for signs of bleeding and inflammation and to rule out other infections which cause symptoms similar to those of IBD.

Endoscopy
In this procedure a long, thin, generally flexible tube (endoscope) with a camera on the tip is used to examine the digestive system. There are different types of endoscopy depending on the area of the body being examined.
An upper GI endoscopy – the endoscope is inserted through the mouth to examine the oesophagus, stomach and duodenum.
A colonoscopy or sigmoidoscopy – a colonoscope (a longer, more flexible endoscope) or a sigmoidoscope (a short endoscope) is inserted through the anus (back passage) to examine the rectum and colon.
Capsule Endoscopy - the patient swallows a capsule containing a tiny camera, transmitter and light source. It takes photos of the inside of the gut as it passes through the system and sends these to a data recorder worn around the waist.
Endoscopies should not be painful but may be uncomfortable so a sedative may be administered to help relax the patient.
Biopsies (small samples of tissue) are often taken during an endoscopy to confirm the diagnosis.

MRI and CT Scans
Magnetic Resonance Imaging (MRI) and Computerised Tomography (CT) are often used to look at the location and extent of inflammation. Occasionally ultrasound scans are used as well.

Barium X-ray
Barium sulphate is a harmless white chalky substance which can be used to coat the lining of the gut and so give a clearer outline in an x-ray. It can be given as a drink or as an enema.

For further and more detailed information about diagnosing IBD please see the Crohn's and Colitis UK leaflet 'Tests and Investigations for IBD'

TREATMENT FOR IBD

Treatment for IBD may be medical, surgical or a combination of both. It depends on the severity and extent of the inflammation and every patient is different. In very mild cases, no treatment may be necessary and occasionally dietary therapy helps to manage the disease.

Drug Treatment
Drug treatment for IBD usually aims to reduce symptoms and control flare ups and then to prevent a relapse once the disease is in remission. The main types of drugs commonly used in IBD are anti-inflammatory drugs and symptomatic drugs.

Anti-inflammatory drugs (help to reduce inflammation)

5-ASAs or amino salicylates such as mesalazine; sulphasalazine; olsalazine and balsalazide.
Corticosteroids (steroids) such as prednisolone; hydrocortisone; budesonide and beclometasone dipropionate.
Immunosuppressants such as azathioprine; mercaptopurine; methotrexate; mycophenolate; mofetil; tacrolimus and ciclosporin.
Biological or 'Anti-TNF' drugs such as infliximab and adalimumab.

Symptomatic drugs (help to control and reduce common symptoms such as pain, diarrhoea and constipation)

Anti-diarrhoeal drugs such as codeine phosphate; diphenoxylate; and Loperamide (Imodium)
Laxatives such as Movicol and Lactulose.
Bulking agents such as Fybogel
Analgesic (pain-killers) such as paracetamol and aspirin.

Antibiotics may be used to treat bacterial infections along with other drug treatments which may become necessary if complications such as anaemia develop.
For further and more detailed information on medical treatments of IBD please see the Crohn's and Colitis UK leaflet 'Drugs used in IBD' and drug information sheets 'Adalimumab, Azathioprine and Mercaptopurine' and 'Methotrexate and Infliximab'.

Surgical Treatment
If a person's quality of life has been affected by repeated 'flare ups' of the disease and they have not responded well to medical treatments surgery may be advised. Surgery may also be advised if dysplasia (pre-cancerous changes) or cancer is found in the bowel. The following are examples of the surgical treatments. The treatment offered to an individual depends on the type and severity of the disease. There are many factors which will influence on how appropriate a surgical option may be.

Proctocolectomy with permanent ileostomy.
In this operation the whole colon, rectum and anal canal are removed and the end of the lower small intestine is brought onto the wall of the abdomen via a permanent opening called a stoma (ileostomy). A bag is placed over the stoma which collects the waste which would have formerly gone from the small intestine into the colon. The bag will need to be emptied and changed when necessary by the patient. This operation will effectively cure the disease as there is no longer a colon to become inflamed and ulcerated. However this is a permanent procedure and reversal is not an option.

Restorative Proctocolectomy with ileoanal pouch.

This is often called pouch surgery, or IPAA (Ileal Pouch-Anal Anastomosis) and is often the preferred surgical option for Ulcerative Colitis. It usually involves two operations, but may occasionally be done in a single stage or in 3 stages.

Stage 1 –the entire colon and rectum is removed but the anus is left in place. A pouch is then created using the lower end of the small intestine. This is attached to the anus. Then the surgeon will create a loop ileostomy using a looped section of the small intestine which is brought out onto the surface of the abdomen. This opening allows the waste from digestion to be collected in a stoma bag until the newly-formed pouch has had a chance to heal. This may take several months.

Stage 2 - the temporary loop ileostomy is closed so the pouch can be used.

Colectomy with ileorectal anastomosis
This operation is much less common. The colon is removed and the end of the small intestine is joined to the rectum. This means a stoma isn't required. This operation can only be performed if there is little or no inflammation in the rectum.

Colectomy with ileostomy (subtotal)
In this procedure involves removing the colon, but leaving the rectum intact. A temporary ileostomy is created. The upper end of the rectum is either closed or brought out to the surface to form another opening or stoma. This additional stoma (sometimes called a mucous fistula) may be needed because the rectum may still produce mucus for a while. This operation means that pouch surgery is a viable option in the future should the patient decide to opt for it. This does depend on the individual's medical condition.

Strictureplasty (stricturoplasty)
Sometimes with Crohn's disease a stricture or narrowing of the intestine occurs. This makes it difficult for food/waste products to pass through and this can lead to blockage. This surgery involves widening the narrowed bowel by opening it up, reshaping it and closing it again. The positive aspect of this surgery is that the patient doesn't have to lose any bowel. If the

stricture is short then it may be possible to dilate the bowel using and endoscopy with a balloon attached to it. This is called an endoscopic dilation. (This surgery is for sufferers of Crohn's disease).

Resection
This involves removing the severely inflamed parts of the intestine, which may have a blockage or a fistula, and then joining the healthy ends together again. (This surgery is for sufferers of Crohn's disease).

Partial colectomy and colostomy
If only the lower part of the colon is damaged by Crohn's disease then this section is removed and the end of the healthy part of the colon is brought onto the surface of the lower left abdomen as a stoma. This is known as a colostomy.

Temporary Ileostomy or Colostomy
The intention of this surgery is to create a stoma to divert the waste away from the affected/inflamed bowel in order to give it a rest and hopefully promote recovery. This will usually be for a period of 3-6 months but will vary depending on the individuals' response and extent of the disease. *For a more detailed explanation of these surgical procedures please see the Crohn's and Colitis UK booklets 'Surgery for Ulcerative Colitis' and 'Surgery for Crohn's Disease'*

DIET AND IBD

There has been a great deal of research into the link between diet and IBD. While it appears that certain foods may lead to 'flare ups' there is little evidence to suggest that diet alone is to blame for developing IBD. It is important for sufferers of IBD to eat a healthy, balanced diet and to take on plenty of fluids to stay hydrated, especially during bouts of diarrhoea. IBD can cause sufferers to become deficient in certain vitamins and minerals such as iron, calcium, vitamin D and vitamin B12 so it may be wise to increase foods rich in these within the diet or to take supplements.

It may be a case of 'trial and error' as to which foods affect each individual. It will become clear quite quickly which foods worsen symptoms and need to be avoided. For example certain foods may cause wind or bloating in some people so it may be wise to avoid these or only eat small amounts. Some people find it better to eat small meals throughout the day rather that one large meal. *For more detailed information about diet and IBD please read the Crohn's and Colitis UK leaflet 'Food and IBD'*

COMPLEMENTARY/ALTERNATIVE THERAPY FOR IBD

Some sufferers of IBD may turn to complementary and alternative medications to help treat or calm some of the symptoms caused by their disease. Some sufferers champion omega 3 fish oils or acupuncture for relieving symptoms. There is a lack of scientific evidence to support alternative medicine in the treatment of IBD and it is suggested that the relief may be the result of a placebo effect. It could also be possible that the disease going into remission at the same time as taking the alternative medications is just a coincidence. It is always advisable to discuss the options with a doctor before embarking on alternative or complementary treatments.

MENTAL WELLBEING

Being diagnosed with a chronic and debilitating condition such as Ulcerative Colitis or Crohn's Disease can be extremely stressful and upsetting. Learning to live with the symptoms takes time and a period of adjustment with many potential obstacles along the way. It is important to take the time to boost mental wellbeing. According to research these five things can really help a person strengthen their coping skills and promote mental health.

Connect – connect with people around you; your family, friends, colleagues and neighbours. Spend time developing these relationships and talking. Joining a support groups to connect with other sufferers of IBD can also be extremely beneficial.

128

Talking to others who understand what it is like to live with the condition can ease the isolation many people feel following diagnosis.

Be active – this doesn't have to mean joining a gym. Research has proven that simply walking for 30 minutes a day can greatly improve mental wellbeing. Or find an activity you enjoy such as cycling or swimming and make it part of your life. Joining an exercise class or walking group is also a good way to connect with people and make new friends.

Keep learning – learning new skills can build confidence and increase self-esteem. Why not sign up for that cookery class or join a choir? You may discover hidden talents and have a great time.

Give to others – even the smallest act can count whether it's just a smile or a kind word. Larger acts such as volunteering at your local community centre can improve mental wellbeing and help you to build new social networks and support groups.

Be mindful – be more aware of the present moment, including your thoughts and feelings, your body and the world around you. Some people call this awareness "mindfulness". It can change the way you feel about life and how you approach challenges and obstacles.

Information courtesy of Crohn's and Colitis UK and www.nhs.uk (2016)

Helpful Websites.
www.depression.org
www.mindful.org-five-steps-to-mindfulness
www.rethink.org
www.time-to-change.org.uk

Useful Organisations

Crohn's and Colitis UK – is a nationwide charity providing a wealth of information and support for sufferers of IBD, their families and much more. This organisation is a lifeline to many and is well worth joining. One of the many benefits of becoming a member is being issued with a 'Can't Wait Card'. This allows access to shops and supermarket lavatory facilities and can be invaluable. It can help to prevent embarrassing accidents occurring as well as giving sufferers of IBD the confidence to get out and about and enjoy life.

> www.crohnsandcolitis.org.uk
> Crohn's and Colitis UK Information Line 08451302233 – open Mon-Fri 10am-1pm.
> Email: info@crohnsandcolitis.org.uk
> Crohn's and Colitis Support 08451303344 – open Mon-Fri 1pm-3.30pm and 6.30pm-9pm

Crohn's and Colitis UK have a huge selection of leaflets and information sheets covering all aspects of IBD which can be downloaded from the website or ordered in print.

Full Crohn's and Colitis UK Publications List
- Understanding IBD – Ulcerative Colitis and Crohn's Disease
- Living with IBD
- Crohn's Disease
- Ulcerative Colitis
- Food and IBD
- Drugs used in IBD
- IBD in children: a parent's guide
- Bones and IBD
- Bowel cancer and IBD
- Children and young people with IBD: a guide for schools

- Counselling for IBD
- Dehydration
- Diarrhoea and Constipation
- Employment and IBD: a guide for employees
- Employment and IBD: a guide for employers
- Fatigue and IBD
- Fertility and IBD
- IBD: a guide for general nurses
- Insurance and IBD
- Living with a Fistula
- Managing Bloating and Wind
- Medical Terms used in IBD
- Microscopic Colitis
- Pregnancy in IBD
- Smoking and IBD
- Staying well with IBD
- Students with IBD: a guide for universities
- Students with IBD: a guide for students
- Surgery for Crohn's Disease
- Surgery for Ulcerative Colitis
- Talking to my child about IBD
- Tests and Investigations for IBD
- Travel and IBD

Drug Treatment Information
- Adalimumab
- Azathioprine and Mercaptopurine
- Infliximab
- Methotrexate
- Azathioprine – for young people
- Methotrexate – for young people

Benefits Guide
- Claiming DLA – Children under 16
- Claiming Personal Independence Payments (PIP)

Other Useful Organisations

Bladder and Bowel Foundation
www.bladderandbowelfoundation.org
0845 345 0165

Colostomy Association
www.colostomyassociation.org.uk
0800 328 4257

Core- Fighting Gut and Liver Disease
www.corecharity.org.uk
020 7486 0341

Crohn's in Childhood Research Association
www.cicra.org
020 8949 6209

IA – The Ileostomy and Internal Pouch Support Group
www.iasupport.org
0800 0184 724

NASS – National Ankylosing Spondylitis Society
www.nass.co.uk
020 8948 9117

National Osteoporosis Society
www.nos.org.uk
0845 450 0230

Ostomy Lifestyle
www.ostomylifestyle.org.uk
0800 731 4264

Glossary of Terms

Abdomen
The part of the body where the stomach, intestines, liver, spleen and pancreas are contained within a cavity lined by peritoneum.

Abscess
A localised collection of pus in the tissues of the body often accompanied by swelling and inflammation and frequently caused by bacteria.

Acid Reflux
A condition which occurs when acid from the stomach flows back up into the oesophagus causing a burning sensation in the chest and sometimes the throat.

Acute
In medicine, an acute disease is one with a rapid onset and/or a short course. The term is used to distinguish a disease from a chronic form which is long-term.

Acute Pancreatitis
A serious condition where the pancreas becomes inflamed over a short period of time. The pancreas is a small organ located behind the stomach and below the ribcage.

Adhesions
An abnormal adhering of surfaces due to inflammation or injury.

Aetiology
The causes or origins of disease.

Anaemia
A deficiency in the number of red blood cells or in their haemoglobin content, resulting in pallor, shortness of breath, and lack of energy.

Anal fissure
A tear or split in the skin around the anus causing bleeding and pain. These may deepen and become termed 'anal ulcers'.

Anal Sphincter
A ring of muscle encircling the anal canal which controls the opening and closing of the anus.

Analgesic
Pain relief or painkiller.

Anastomosis
The surgical joining of two ends of bowel following a resection.

Antibiotic
Drugs used to fight bacterial infections.

Anti-diarrhoeals
Medications used to 'firm up' stools (faeces) and treat diarrhoea.

Anus (back passage)
The opening at the bottom end of the GI tract, at the end of the rectum.

Arthritis
Inflammation of a joint causing stiffness of movement, pain and swelling.

Bacteria - microscopic organisms. Some may cause infection; others can be helpful in digestion and in destroying other harmful organisms.

Barium Enema/Meal
A procedure used to examine the colon. A white liquid which contains barium is put into the colon through the anus. This coats the lining of the bowel which gives a clearer X-ray. The barium liquid can also be drunk to coat the esophagus stomach and small intestine for the same purpose.

Bile
A fluid produced by the liver and stored in the gall bladder which helps to digest fat.

Biopsy
A small piece of tissue taken from the body for microscopic examination.

Blood test
A scientific examination of a sample of blood, typically for the diagnosis of illness or for the detection and measurement of drugs or other substances.

Bowels
Also known as intestines.

Caecum
The first section of the colon, located in the lower right of the abdomen.

Capsule Endoscopy
An investigation to examine the digestive system using a small capsule containing a minute camera which is swallowed. The images are transmitted to a data recorder worn by the patient. The capsule will pass out of the body naturally in a bowel movement.

Chest Infection
An infection that affects the lungs, either in the larger airways (bronchitis) or in the smaller air sacs (pneumonia). There is a build-up of pus and fluid (mucus), and the airways become swollen, making breathing difficult.

Chronic
An ongoing or continuous disease or illness lasting months or years.

Colon
Also known as the large intestine.

Colonoscopy
A procedure by which a colonoscope (thin tube with a camera on the end) is inserted through the anus to examine the rectum and colon.

Colostomy
A surgical operation where the cut end of the colon is brought out onto the abdomen to create an opening called a stoma. A disposable bag is placed over the stoma in order to collect the digestive waste. A colostomy may be temporary or permanent.

Constipation
Difficulty in passing stools due to them becoming hard, dry and painful to pass.

Consultant
A hospital doctor of senior rank within a specific field

Corticosteroids
A drug treatment to help control the symptoms and disease process of IBD. Also known as steroids.

Crohn's Colitis
Crohn's disease within the colon.

CT scan (Computerised Tomography)
A type of X-ray looking a cross sections of the body.

Crohns disease

A long-term condition that causes inflammation of the lining of the digestive system. The inflammation can affect any part of the digestive system, from the mouth to the back passage, but most commonly occurs in the last section of the small intestine (ileum) or the large intestine (colon).

Deep Vein Thrombosis (DVT)
A blood clot in one of the deep veins in the body.

Defaecation
Passing stool or faeces.

Dehydration
A condition which occurs if too much liquid is lost from the body through diarrhoea, vomiting or not taking on enough fluids.

Depression
A mood disorder that causes a persistent feeling of sadness and loss of interest. Also called major depression, major depressive disorder or clinical depression.

Diarrhoea
A condition in which faeces are discharged from the bowels frequently and in a liquid form.

Dietician
A qualified professional trained to advise and educate people about a healthy and appropriate diet.

Dilated
Widened.

Distal or left-sided colitis
Inflammation that travels up the left side of the colon, but doesn't reach the top/ right side.

Distension
Gas and fluid in the abdomen causing a swollen uncomfortable pressure.

Diverticular disease
Small bulges or pouches, called diverticula which develop in the wall of the colon. This is termed diverticulitis if they become inflamed or infected.

Duodenum
The first part of the small intestine.

Dysplasia

A change in the appearance of microscopic cells lining the gastrointestinal tract which is an early indication of the possible development of cancer.

Electrolytes
Salts in the blood, such as sodium, potassium and calcium.

Endoscopy
Refers to looking inside the body for medical reasons using an **endoscope**, a thin tube with a camera on the tip used to examine the interior of a hollow organ or cavity of the body. Unlike most other medical imaging devices, endoscopes are inserted directly into the organ.

Enema
A procedure in which liquid or gas is injected into the rectum, to expel its contents or to introduce drugs or permit X-ray imaging.

Enteral nutrition
A specially designed, highly nutritional liquid food is taken by mouth or passed into the stomach through a nasogastric tube (a fine flexible tube inserted through the nose).

Enteritis
Inflammation of the small intestine.

ESR (Erythrocyte Sedimentation Rate)
A blood test used to measure inflammation in the body.

Exacerbation
A worsening of symptoms or an increase in the activity of the disease often referred to as a relapse or a 'flare-up'.

Faecal calprotectin
Specific proteins found in the stools (faeces). When levels of these proteins increase this can indicate inflammation.

Faeces (stools, motions)
Waste matter from digestion passed out through the anus or stoma.

Fatigue
Persistent physical or mental exhaustion that isn't relieved through sleep.

FBC (full blood count)
A blood test that measures red blood cell count, white cell count and platelet count. Used to detect inflammation and anaemia, and also for monitoring patients on long-term medication.

Fistula
An abnormal passage connecting two loops of intestine, or the intestine to another organ or to the skin.

Flare Up
When the symptoms of IBD return and the disease becomes active again.

Flatus
Gas from the stomach or bowels let out through the rectum or stoma. Also known as wind.

Folic acid or folate
A vitamin that is essential for forming red blood cells. Poor diet or poor absorption by the small intestine can result if this vitamin is lacking.

Gastroenterologist
A doctor who is specially trained in the field of intestinal disorders, including IBD.

Gastrointestinal Tract (GI)
An organ system responsible for consuming and digesting foodstuffs, absorbing nutrients, and expelling waste. The tract consists of the stomach and intestines, and is divided into the upper and lower gastrointestinal tracts

Gastroscopy
An examination of the oesophagus, stomach and duodenum, using a thin tube with a camera in its tip, (gastroscope), which is inserted through the mouth.

Genetics
The study of how individuals inherit physical and behavioural characteristics and medical conditions from their parents. Genetics are believed to be one of the causative factors in developing IBD.

Generalised anxiety disorder
A psychological disorder characterized by excessive or disproportionate anxiety about several aspects of life, such as work, social relationships, or financial matters.

General Practitioner (GP)
A medical doctor who treats acute and chronic illnesses and provides preventive care and health education to patients.

Gut
The digestive system or gastrointestinal tract.

Haemoglobin

A substance found in red blood cells that transports oxygen around the body.

Haemorrhoids (piles)
Swollen veins in or around the anus which can bleed and cause pain.

Hydrocortisone
A steroid drug, which reduces inflammation.

IBD
Inflammatory Bowel Disease.

IBD nurse
A specialist nurse in the field of IBD who can provide support and advice for people affected by IBD.

Ileal pouch-anal anastomosis (IPAA)
A surgical procedure where a pouch is made from the ileum following removal of the colon. The end of the pouch is attached to the anus enabling the patient to pass stools via the anus and eliminates the need for a stoma. Also known as restorative proctocolectomy or 'j-pouch'

Ileocaecal valve
A valve at the joining of the small and large intestines that prevents food residue flowing back to the ileum from the colon.

Ileorectal anastomosis
A surgical operation for IBD after removal of the colon. The end of the ileum is attached to the rectum.

Ileostomy
A surgically created opening into part of the small bowel (called the ileum), which is then brought out at skin level (called a stoma). There are essentially two types of ileostomy: end ileostomy and loop ileostomy.

Ileostomy bag
A special bag is placed over the stoma to collect waste products that would usually pass through the colon (large intestine) and out of the body through the rectum and anus (back passage).

Ileum
The lower part of the small intestine, which joins the colon at the ileocaecal valve. Inflammation of the ileum is known as ileitis.

Immune system
The body's defence system against infections or other harmful disease causing organisms. It responds by recognising and attacking antigens.

Impacted bowel
A solid, immobile bulk of human faeces that can develop in the rectum as a result of chronic constipation.

Incontinence
Unintentional passing or leakage of stools and/or urine.

Inflammation
The body's response to irritation, infection or injury. Blood gathers in affected areas leading to reddening, swelling and pain.

Informed Consent
Permission granted in full knowledge of the possible consequences, typically that which is given by a patient to a doctor for treatment with knowledge of the possible risks and benefits.

Infusion
A procedure to inject a liquid directly into the blood stream. The fluid flows from a sterile bag through plastic tubing through a small needle into a vein.

Intramuscular (IM)
Into a muscle.

Intravenously (IV)
Into a vein.

Jejunum
The section of small bowel between the duodenum and the ileum.

Laparoscopy (key=hole surgery)
A surgical procedure in which a lighted instrument called a laparoscope is passed through a small cut in the abdominal wall to examine internal organs or to carry out surgery.

Large intestine
Colon

Laxative
A substance that helps to clear the bowel.

Lesion
Damage or injury to tissue anywhere in the body.

Leucocytes/leukocytes
White cells in the blood which help to fight infection.

LFTs (liver function tests)
Blood tests to ascertain how well the liver is functioning by measuring specific proteins and enzymes in the blood.

Liver
The largest gland in the body with many functions the main one being regulate blood chemicals.

Loop Ileostomy
Performed as part of an operation whereby a portion of the large bowel is removed and the two ends are joined together (anastomosis). The ileostomy in these circumstances is formed to allow the join in the bowel to heal for a few months, and is only a temporary measure.

Maintenance therapy
Usually drug treatment taken long-term to keep an illness in remission.

Malabsorption
The failure to fully absorb the nutrients in food through the intestines. Malabsorption may result in malnutrition.

Mesalazine
The generic name for one of the 5-aminosalicylic acid (5 ASA) group of drugs. Brand names include Asacol, Ipocol, Mesren, Mezavant XL, Pentasa, Octasa and Salofalk.

Moon facies
A condition which may cause the face to gradually become round, full, or puffy due to long-term use of steroid medications.

Morphine
An analgesic and narcotic drug obtained from opium and used medicinally to relieve pain.

Morphine Pump/Patient Controlled Analgesia (PCA)
Any method of allowing a person in pain to administer their own pain relief. In a hospital setting a PCA refers to an electronically controlled infusion pump that delivers an amount of intravenous analgesic when the patient presses a button.

Motility
The contraction of muscles in the intestinal tract.

MRI (magnetic resonance imaging) scan

An examination of internal organs using strong magnets and radio waves rather than x-rays. Therefore no radiation is used.

MRI enteroclysis/enterography
Types of MRI test used to assess the small and large bowel using a gas or liquid to give clearer images. Enteroclysis – gas/liquid passed into intestine via a tube. Enterography – the liquid is drunk

Mucus Fistula
Is formed when the two ends of the bowel are bought out onto the surface of the abdomen. One is formed to pass the faeces and the other to release mucous produced by the disconnected end of the bowel.

Nausea
A feeling of sickness in the stomach characterized by an urge to vomit.

Nil by Mouth (NBM)
A medical order that prohibits anyone from giving a patient food, drink, or medications by mouth.

NSAIDs (non-steroidal anti-inflammatory drugs)
Painkillers often used for arthritis, such as ibuprofen and diclofenac. There is some evidence that they may make IBD worse.

Obsessive-compulsive disorder (OCD)
A psychological disorder characterized by unreasonable thoughts and fears (obsessions) that lead you to do repetitive behaviors (compulsions). It's also possible to have only obsessions or only compulsions and still have OCD.

Obstruction
A blockage of the small or large intestine.

Occult blood
Blood in the stool that can only be detected by laboratory analysis.

Oedema
Swelling caused by the gathering of fluid in the tissues.

Oesophagus (gullet)
The part of the digestive system from the throat to the stomach down which food passes.

Oral Crohn's
Crohn's Disease in the mouth.

Osteoporosis

Thinning of the bones that may result in weakness and an increased risk of fractures. It is more prevalent in IBD sufferers than in the general population. Contributory factors include long-term use of corticosteroids, severe active disease or by oestrogen levels.

Ostomy (see stoma)
An artificial opening of the intestine onto the wall of the abdomen.

Paediatrician
A specialist doctor in the care of children and young people.

Parenteral nutrition
A method of giving a specially prepared liquid food into a vein when nutrient absorption through the intestines is compromised.

Pathogen
A harmful disease causing organism, such as a bacterium or virus.

Pathology
The study of disease, its causes and progression by examining samples of tissue, blood, stool and urine.

Perforation
An abnormal opening in the bowel wall which results in the contents of the bowel to leak into the abdominal cavity.

Perianal
The area around the anus.

Peristalsis
The wave-like muscle contractions that move food through the digestive system.

Peritoneum
The membrane lining the inside of the abdominal cavity.

Physiotherapist
A health care professional who assists people affected by injury, illness or disability through movement and exercise, manual therapy, education and advice.

Pouch (ileo-anal)
An internal pouch or reservoir constructed from the lower part of the intestine (ileum) which is joined to the anus. This allows stools to pass out through the anus in the usual way.

Pouchitis
Inflammation of an ileo-anal pouch.

Prebiotic
A non-digestible food ingredient that promotes the growth of beneficial microorganisms in the intestines.

Preeclampsia
A serious pregnancy complication usually beginning after 20 weeks gestation characterized by high blood pressure and signs of damage to another organ system, often the kidneys.

Pre-medication
A drug treatment given to a patient before a (surgical or invasive) medical procedure. These drugs are typically sedative or analgesic.

Probiotics
A substance which stimulates the growth of microorganisms, especially those with beneficial properties (healthy bacteria) in the gut.

Proctitis
Inflammation in the rectum.

Proctocolectomy (total colectomy)
The surgical removal of the colon and rectum.

Proctosigmoiditis
Inflammation of the rectum and lower colon.

Prognosis
A prediction of the likely progress of the disease.

Prophylactic therapy
Preventive treatment.

Pus
A thick yellowish or greenish opaque liquid produced in infected tissue, consisting of dead white blood cells and bacteria with tissue debris and serum.

Radiologist
A physician trained in the diagnostic and/or therapeutic use of x-rays; a diagnostic radiologist is trained in diagnostic ultrasound and magnetic resonance imaging.

Rectal bleeding

Blood passed from the anus.

Rectum
The last part of the colon.

Red blood cells or erythrocytes
Blood cells containing haemoglobin, which carry oxygen from the lungs to the tissues and return carbon dioxide to the lungs.

Relapse
Return of disease activity after it has been inactive. Often called a 'flare-up'.

Remission
Prolonged periods of time without symptoms or active disease.

Resection
The surgical removal of a part of the intestine.

Right hemicolectomy
An operation to remove the terminal ileum and caecum.

Septicaemia
Blood poisoning caused by bacteria and their toxins.

Scan
A medical examination using a scanner.

Sigmoid colon
The s-shaped lower end of the colon, leading into the rectum.

Sigmoidoscopy
A short tube with a camera in its tip (sigmoidoscope) is inserted through the anus to examine to examine the lower part of the colon and the rectum.

Small intestine
The section of the intestines responsible for digesting food and absorbing nutrients. The small intestine has three regions:
Upper - the duodenum
Middle - the jejunum
Lower - the ileum

Specialised Stoma Care Nurse
A nurse specialised in the area of stoma care.

Steroids
See *corticosteroids*.

Stoma
A surgically created opening of the intestine onto the abdominal wall, over which a bag can be attached.

Stoma Cap
A round flat bag used to collect the mucous produced by a mucous fistula.

Stools
Motions, faeces, poo.

Stricture
Occurs when a section of the bowel becomes narrowed due to bowel wall thickening, inflammation or scarring.

Strictureplasty
An operation to widen a narrow section of the bowel.

Supra Pubic Catheter
A catheter (tube) which drains urine from the bladder. It is inserted into the bladder through a small hole in the abdomen.

Surgical Drain
A tube used to remove pus, blood or other fluids from a wound.

Suppository
A solid medical preparation in a roughly conical or cylindrical shape, designed to be inserted into the rectum or vagina to dissolve.

Sutures
Stitches.

Tenesmus
Inflammation in the rectum resulting in a persistent urge to empty the bowel.

Terminal ileum
The last part of the small intestine before it joins the large intestine.

Total Colectomy
The removal of the large intestine from the lowest part of the small intestine (ileum) to the rectum.

Toxic megacolon
Widening or swelling of the colon which may cause perforation.

Transition

The stage at which a young person moves from paediatric (child) health care to adult health care usually between the ages of 14-18

Tumour
An abnormal growth which may be benign (non-cancerous) or malignant (cancerous).

U&E (urea and electrolytes)
A blood test which mainly checks kidney function.

Ulcer
An open sore on external or internal tissues of the body.

Ulcerative Colitis
A long term, chronic condition, where the colon and rectum become inflamed. Small ulcers can develop on the lining of the colon, and can bleed and produce pus.

Ultrasound scan
A painless test that uses sound waves to create images of organs and structures inside the body.

Viruses
Very small infection causing organisms which invade and multiply within other cells.

Vitamin D
A vitamin essential for the health of bonesproduction depends on exposure to sunlight on the skin.

X-ray
A photographic or digital image of the internal composition of something, especially a part of the body.

The above information is to help explain some of the terms and procedures associated with IBD. Not all of the terms are found within the content of this book.

18542101R00093

Printed in Poland
by Amazon Fulfillment
Poland Sp. z o.o., Wrocław